Bach's Passions

Passio Domini nostri J. C. secundum Evangelistam Matthæum

Presà per Dominum Henrici alias Picander dictus.

Musica di G. S. Bach.

Prima Parte.

41.5.

Title-page of autograph score of Bach's St Matthew Passion.

Masterworks of Choral Music

Bach's Passions

Paul Steinitz

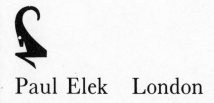

Paul Elek   London

To my Daughter

First published 1979 by
Paul Elek Limited
54–58 Caledonian Road London N1 9RN

Copyright © 1979 by Paul Steinitz

On the endpapers and as frontispiece are reproduced pages from the
facsimile autograph score *Johann Sebastian Bach: Matthäus-Passion,*
BWV 244, edited by Karl-Heinz Köhler, 2nd ed., ©1974 by VEB
Deutscher Verlag für Musik Leipzig

ISBN 0 236 40132 7

Printed in Great Britain by
Unwin Brothers Limited
The Gresham Press
Old Woking, Surrey

Contents

Preface

Many years of teaching students and training amateur choralists have convinced me that there is a need for a book on the Bach Passions which gives their historical background, discusses the music, and sketches a brief account of performance practice since Bach's time all under one cover.

This book is primarily designed to help music-lovers from amateur choralists to students at school or college to increase their enjoyment of singing in or listening to Bach's Passion music through an understanding of its place in musical history and by studying it. This does not rule out the more general reader, but the book will be most useful to those who have at least some knowledge of music and musical terms. Access to scores of the two Passions is also important. References are based on the Neue Bach Ausgabe full scores, but may be followed up from any unabridged vocal score that may be to hand. It should be mentioned, however, that the standard English vocal score gives a distorted version of Bach's notes and rhythms, especially in the recitatives, in its effort to preserve the words of the Authorized Version. One of the objects of this book is to make points that are missed in this version; reference to any available German version, miniature or vocal score, will help in this connection. Similarly, the text in English editions is often at variance with Bach's musical intentions; in quotations I therefore give the original German with its equivalent in English.

In dealing with the music itself I have deliberately avoided the kind of structural analysis which has little immediate relationship to general understanding and enjoyment. Such analysis too often creates boredom instead of achieving the enlightenment which is intended. This means, for example, that I have adopted no consistent pattern of analysing/describing the harmony, keys and rhythm of each chorus and aria. Music students and others for whom such analysis is important are encouraged to do it for themselves. They will find various hints in this direction and suggestions as to how to pursue study at a deeper level scattered throughout the book. The Bibliography may be found useful for this purpose too.

I have resisted pressure from musicological friends and advisors to develop to any length matters which could be of interest only to a tiny minority of readers. For this reason I have kept to a minimum space given, for example, to earlier Passions, and to ideas about the redating of movements and of first performances that various scholars have put forward during the last twenty years or so. I am not minimizing the importance to performers that new datings could have in regard to details of notation, instrumentation and even style, if they indicated great divergences from those generally accepted at present. But conclusions on such matters, being constantly changing, are difficult to accept finally, and in any case, this book is not primarily concerned with performance practice.

In short, I have not set out to add to the enormous amount of scholarship that already exists on the subject of the Passions, but rather to try to interest the reader by giving the general background of the music and my own reactions to it.

I have drawn heavily on C.S. Terry's *Bach's Chorales*, Part I (on those used in the Passions) for the factual information given in the Appendix, and on F. Blume's *Protestant Church Music* for what is said about Pietism in Chapter 4.

For English versions of quotations from the biblical passages in the Passions, the Authorized Version has been used; for chorales and free text numbers a translation which is as close as possible has been given.

I am indebted to a large number of people for help in preparing this book, chiefly the following: Cecilia Bezer and Beverley Luyt for typing, Elizabeth Glasser for her part in the preparation of the music examples, Antony Wood of Paul Elek Limited and Peter Dodd for much good advice, the orchestral librarian at the Royal Academy of Music for making Henry Wood's scores and parts available, Michael Pipe of Goldsmiths' College and John Haberlen of Georgia State University for sundry information, Erna Frank for translation of some obscure passages, Messrs J.M. Dent & Sons Ltd and W.W. Norton & Company, Inc. for their permission to quote a passage from *The Bach Reader* by David and Mendel (see Bibliography), and my wife Margaret for help with the discography and for her patience during my long periods of preoccupation.

P.S.

1
The German Passion
Tradition Before Bach

The following description of Bach leading an ensemble was
written by a close colleague, Johann Mattias Gesner, rector of
the Thomaskirche, Leipzig, between 1730 and 1734:

You would think but slightly, my dear Fabius, of all these [the
accomplishments of the citharists of the underworld], if you could see
Bach... either playing our clavier, which is many citharas in one, with
all the fingers of both hands, or running over the keys of the instrument
of instruments... with both hands and, at the utmost speed, with his
feet, producing by himself the most various and at the same time
mutually agreeable combinations of sounds in orderly procession. If you
could see him, I say, doing what many of your citharists and six
hundred of your tibia players together could not do, not only... singing
with one voice and playing his own part, but watching over everything
and bringing back to the rhythm and the beat, out of thirty or even
forty musicians, the one with a nod, another by tapping with his foot,
the third with a warning finger, giving the right note to one from the
top of his voice, to another from the bottom and to a third from the
middle of it—all alone, in the midst of the greatest din made by all the
participants, and, although he is executing the most difficult parts
himself, noticing at once whenever and wherever a mistake occurs,
holding everyone together, taking precautions everywhere, and repairing
any unsteadiness, full of rhythm in every part of his body—this one
man taking in all these harmonies with his keen ear and emitting with
his voice alone the tone of all the voices. Favourer as I am of antiquity,
the accomplishments of our Bach, and of any others that there may be
like him, appear to me to effect what not many Orpheuses, nor twenty
Arions, could achieve.[1]

Arthur Mendel states that there may have been a performance
of Bach's St John Passion around 1730, the first year of Gesner's
rectorship at the Thomaskirche. So the above could possibly
describe Bach directing a Passion rehearsal.

The name of Bach is intimately linked with the whole experience of performing and listening to Passion music, and it would not be surprising if some imagined that he invented the form as well as the music of his settings; it is only comparatively recently that articles and books on earlier Passions have appeared in English, and that much interest has been shown in these works. The first examples of the form in fact go back about five hundred years.

The idea of chanting the story of Christ's Passion during Holy Week goes back many hundreds of years to the time when the Gospel story appointed by the Church for the day was sung by the priest so that the voice carried better than in speech in large resonant buildings.

In medieval times each voice part carried certain indications as to style of performance: for example, the words of the Evangelist (narrator) had *C* (*celeriter*), that is in a flowing style, and those of Jesus *T* (*tenere*), in other words rather slower or held back. By tradition, the main narration was sung by a tenor, the part of Jesus by a bass and from the fifteenth century onwards, all other parts, including the crowd, by a high (alto) voice. This custom persisted well into the seventeenth century. In Holy Week these recitations of the Passion story in Latin were appointed as follows: Palm Sunday, St Matthew, Chapters 26 and 27; Tuesday, St Mark, Chapters 14 and 15; Wednesday, St Luke, Chapters 22 and 23; and Good Friday, St John, Chapters 18 and 19.

In the first 'composed' settings, that is to say, ones in which music other than the traditional plainsong was also used, a chorus sang the part of the crowd (called *turba*); it represented the priests and scribes or the mass of the people, and so on; the chorus could be in three, four or more voice parts. Its sudden entry during the course of the chanting of the story naturally made a dramatic effect, and this type of setting is known as the Dramatic or Liturgical Passion; either title fits it well. Settings of this type, which were always unaccompanied, sprang from the pens of composers working in widely separated areas during the sixteenth century, for example Victoria in Spain, Davy[2] and then Byrd in England, and Lassus in the Netherlands. These were of course in the Roman tradition, and their purpose was not primarily to make a direct impact on the congregation. In Germany, the Reformation took root during the third decade of the sixteenth century, earlier than elsewhere. In 1524 the first book of hymns or chorales in the vernacular appeared (see Chapter 4 under *Chorales*). The results of this, coupled with Luther's translation of the Bible into German, can hardly be over-estimated, or indeed fully understood at this distance of time. But by the middle of the century the effect on composers of Passions, who naturally set Luther's Bible (as did J.S. Bach nearly two hundred years later), was to make them write music easily intelligible to the people, who were by then expecting to hear and understand the words. Intelligibility was achieved through clear and simple textures, mainly with one note to a syllable, in contrast to the more melismatic style of the Roman tradition and to the rhythmically more lively style of, for instance, the *turba* choruses in Byrd's late sixteenth-century Latin setting of St John's account of the Passion.[3] A link with the past in early settings, for example Johann Walther's of 1530, was the retention as *cantus firmus* or basis for the choral as well as the other sections, of traditional plainsong melodies; but these were treated freely. A definitive version of the melodies associated with Passions, called Passion Tones, was published in Rome in 1586.

Although these Dramatic Passions flourished chiefly in the sixteenth century, they persisted until 1666, the last setting being Schütz's St Matthew. The text was entirely biblical, apart from opening and closing choruses; the words of the former were usually 'This is' or 'Hear Ye', continuing, say, 'the Passion according to St Matthew' or 'St John'; the latter drew a moral, often in the words of a hymn. Remnants of this tradition greatly enlarged and altered can be seen in the Passions of J.S. Bach.

During the sixteenth century, a new type of setting developed, in which the entire story, including all the different characters and the crowd, was given to a chorus. This is known as the Motet Passion. Its weakness was its unrealistic quality; on the other hand, personalities in the form of soloists were avoided. Again, the Passion Tones were often used as a *cantus firmus* round which the other voices weaved a polyphonic thread. Leonhardt Lechner (d.1606)[4] composed a beautiful example; the last known setting was by Christoph Demantius in 1630.[5] These are occasionally heard today. Besides pure examples of Dramatic Passions and Motet Passions, many works were composed in the sixteenth and early seventeenth centuries which show a varying amount of choral setting of words other than those of the crowd and a varying amount of use of plainsong.

The seventeenth century saw further changes in the style of Passions, with the gradual moving away from plainchant, the introduction of instruments, and the interpolation of non-biblical texts, variously set, commenting on the story and drawing morals or lessons in the manner which is so familiar to us in Bach's works. This more sectional structure, with its increased emphasis on characterization through instrumental colour, had a parallel in the oratorios which emerged in Italy about the same time. Hence this type of Passion is known as the Oratorio Passion. These changes, which were so fundamental that the style from which they developed was actually called 'the New Music', came about as a result of the attitudes towards music and its function which grew up in Italy around 1600. Composers turned away from the complicated textures of polyphony, the language of the sixteenth century, and in evolving a style mainly suitable for opera, developed recitative, or monody, a way of setting mainly secular words to music for a single voice and instrumental bass; this was regarded as a form of 'heightened speech'. In other words, composers believed that the natural inflection of language should govern both the rhythm and melodic outline of the vocal part. Between the bass—called *basso continuo*—and the voice part, harmonies were played on a keyboard instrument, thus filling in the basic two-part texture. Here was the direct antecedent of Bach's Passion recitatives.

As a result of the movement away from many-voiced textures, in which available instruments simply doubled or supplanted voices, the chance now presented itself of instruments playing independent parts; at the same time stringed instruments themselves developed partly because of the new opportunities offered, and partly owing to very fine makers, working mainly in Italy, who flourished about this time. Woodwind were slightly slower in developing and the orchestral oboe, for instance, does not appear until about the middle of the seventeenth century.

This expansion of musical and textural resources was a gradual process in that not all the possible—and now familiar—non-biblical elements and obbligato instruments were introduced at once. Thus one setting might include some familiar and seasonal hymn verses only, another freely composed verses, and these could be variously allocated to solo voices or chorus or both, with or without instruments. One of the most interesting and musically rewarding examples of this type is Thomas Selle's St John Passion (Hamburg, 1643),[6] although the liturgical (i.e. biblical) sections are somewhat stiffly set. The characters are each associated with their own instrumental group, a practice which is very much in the tradition of the seventeenth and eighteenth centuries, but which was dropped later (Bach did not follow it, except in his St Matthew Passion, and then only with the voice of Jesus). Thus the Evangelist has two bassoons, Jesus two violins and one bassoon, and so on. The choice of instruments is related absolutely to the doctrine of 'Affections', a theory fundamental to baroque composition which associated moods, scenes, emotional states and certain classes of people with certain kinds of melodic shapes and rhythms and instruments. Thus brass, and especially trumpets, were associated with royalty, so Pilate, as the Emperor's representative, has cornetts (not brass, but often associated with brass instruments) and a trombone. This rule was not always strictly followed by composers of the time, on the other hand it was sometimes followed to an exaggerated degree, as will be shown in a later chapter. Musically, the finest sections of Selle's Passions are the big interpolated choruses: 'Surely he hath born our griefs', 'My God, my God, why hast Thou forsaken me?', and the chorale 'O guiltless Lamb of God'. These are scored for solo soprano, tenor and bass, solo violin, strings, bassoons, continuo and five-part chorus. The music is daringly impassioned in places.

Most other seventeenth-century Oratorio Passions, with the exception of one work of Schütz, tend to be interesting for historical reasons only. They show the use of strings accompanying the words of Jesus (though not always), and varied types of interpolation including sinfonias. The intrinsic quality of the Passions of Sebastiani (Königsberg, 1672),[7] Theile (Lübeck, 1673)[8] and Funcke (Lüneberg, 1683)[9] is not great; in fact, very often their work is appallingly dull. No Oratorio Passion was composed in Leipzig until Kuhnau's St Mark Passion of 1721, only a year or two before Bach's St John Passion and eight years before his St Matthew. This fact is important for the understanding of the Leipzig people's reaction to Bach's Passions, of which something will be said in a later chapter. It is explained by the further fact that Leipzig congregations were conservative in their attitude to a more secular and dramatic style of church music and, despite the town's position as an important centre of Lutheran orthodoxy, did not know much about what went on in other towns. At the time of his appointment at Leipzig Bach was asked to 'make compositions that were not theatrical'.[10]

This brings us to the contribution made by Heinrich Schütz (1585–1672) to the development of Passion Music.

Schütz is now recognized as one of the greatest composers of the seventeenth century, indeed of all time. He spent almost the whole of his working life at the court of the Elector of Saxony in Dresden, and even when he became very old and wished to retire, his employers held him in such high esteem that they were reluctant to release him from his duties completely, and wished him to continue to exert some influence on music at court. Schütz's fame rests on the miraculous way in which as a result of his 'study' visits to Italy, he managed to combine the most exciting characteristics of the 'New Music' of that country (see above) and also the polychoral style (namely music for several separated groups of musicians) of St Mark's, Venice with whose musical director, Giovanni Gabrieli, he studied, with the rather severe features of German music. However, in his Passion music he chose to eschew any hint of secular influences from Italy or anywhere else. In fact he composed only four Passion settings, and only one of these, *The Seven Last Words*[11], could be said to have affected the course of history. This concise and beautiful piece sets the story in a composite version, drawn from all four Gospels, for chorus, five voices, various instruments and continuo. Four of the soloists provide Evangelists of varied timbre and pitch, and the fifth, tenor 2, sings the part of Jesus. From its austere style one gets the impression that Schütz regarded anything florid or extrovert as unsuitable for such a solemn subject; in fact, of this work it could well be said that never has so much been expressed by so few notes and such simple resources. Very late in life, Schütz composed three fine but also somewhat austere Dramatic Passions: St Luke (1665), St John (1666) and St Matthew (1666), thus reverting to a form popular nearly one hundred years earlier. The reason for this swing back to a much earlier style is that at that time in the Dresden court chapel instruments were silent during Lent. Thus although Schütz's

Passions are sometimes referred to as forerunners of J.S. Bach's, traces of their influence on the latter are minimal, save in the case of *The Seven Last Words*.

Although he did not compose examples of the kind himself, the Passion Oratorios which emerged in Hamburg about the turn of the seventeenth and eighteenth centuries were the most immediate influence on Bach. Oratorios based on the Passion story, not settings of it, these were an extension of the sacred operas which were popular in that city (the first opera house opened in 1678 with a work based on the story of Adam and Eve by Theile). In this kind of work the Gospel words were versified and rhymed by poets who exploited to excess, through a multitude of original interpolations reflecting on the story, the more gruesome aspects of the Passion. In so doing they used colourful imagery which fired the imagination of every important composer of the day, including J.S. Bach, who used words from one of the most famous Passion Oratorio libretti, by Barthold Heinrich Brockes, *Der für die Sünden der Welt gemarterte und sterbende Jesus*, in his St John Passion.

A word must now be said about religious and musical conditions in Leipzig during and immediately preceding the time Bach composed his Passions. The Thirty Years War (1618–48) caused such devastation in Central Germany that its effects reached well into the eighteenth century. Not only were musical establishments broken up but music itself was affected, its chosen texts tending to look forward to escaping from the storms of this world to the peace of the next. Shortly after this, and probably to some degree as a result of it, came the spread of the movement known as Pietism.

As Lutheran orthodoxy became increasingly severe in its emphasis that salvation could be found only in the Sacraments, the Bible and the Sermon, and at a time when the Church was losing its authority under the impact of French-inspired rationalism, a reaction set in. In the generation before Bach's birth, Philipp Jakob Spener began to pursue a Christianity of experience and action, teaching that Sacraments, Holy Scripture and Sermon were not enough, that instead 'the wide dissemination of the Word of God, the deepening of personal piety and the practice of the priesthood of all believers were necessary for salvation'[12]. Pietism became a popular movement, filled with spiritual warmth, emphasizing ethical values, reshaping daily life with devotions, catechisms, simple hymns and sacred songs of a mystical and emotional nature in the home. The adherents of Pietism were against elaborate church music of the sort being developed everywhere towards the end of the seventeenth century.

The clash between Pietism and Lutheran orthodoxy lasted through the closing third of the seventeenth and the first half of the eighteenth centuries, but there was much interpenetration and amalgamation of the two, the effect of Pietism being felt in circles that strongly opposed it, and both streams of thought often using the same language. In Halle, only a few miles from Leipzig, another side of the Pietist movement was unleashed by the intolerant, aggressive August Hermann Francke, who cultivated an overemotional bliss that 'dwelt inexhaustibly on a mysticism of ardent pain and ecstasy'.[13]

In Leipzig in Bach's time, the impact of Pietism, especially in its Halle variety, was strong, and permeated both Bach's thinking and his librettists'. This impact led to what was virtually a conflict between orthodox Lutheranism, with its long tradition of music as an essential part of worship, and the simple devotional life of Pietism. On the other hand, it must also be mentioned that, whereas this dichotomy is evident in the texts which Bach set, there is a theory current in some circles today, based on a redating of Bach's religious compositions at Leipzig, that since during the third decade of the eighteenth century he virtually gave up the regular writing of church music, he had become disillusioned not only about the conditions of performance but also about religion itself.*

In Bach's time all musicians, including composers, were employed either by noblemen for their court and chapel music or by municipal authorities in the secular field or for music in churches, where composers might be cantors or organists. All music was written for a specific and immediate purpose, and nearly everything performed, therefore, was new.

Since the fifteenth century the Imperial Diet had consisted of three chambers: the Colleges of Electors; Princes, Barons, and Counts; and the Imperial Free Cities. Leipzig was one of these Free Cities and therefore did not have the advantage of a court orchestra. Instead, the professional *Stadtpfeifer* (town musicians)

* This subject is dealt with in slightly more detail in Chapter 5.

combined with amateurs to form church orchestras. Those who worked for city councils supplied music for both sacred and secular occasions. The varying size, composition and skill of these choirs and orchestras can to some extent be assessed from the scoring of the music written for them. Choirs and orchestras balanced each other in size, the orchestras being if anything slightly larger than the choirs. It is very difficult to form an accurate opinion of standards, which evidently varied enormously with the size and status of the court or town. However, we may quote here Bach's own comments, made in 1730, about some of his Leipzig players: 'Modesty forbids me to speak at all truthfully about their qualities and musical knowledge.'[14] It is worth noting that it is unlikely that some of his most difficult woodwind music (e.g. the Flute Suite) was written for these players.[15]

This then was the world in which J.S. Bach worked when he composed his settings of the Passions.

2
The Baroque Style of Composition

Although there must be almost as much baroque music performed today as during the period in which it was written, the ordinary listener may still not understand why it sounds or should sound so utterly different from that with which he is most familiar; that is to say, the music of composers from Mozart to those of the early twentieth century. It differs most widely from compositions of the nineteenth century, and these still provide the major part of public concert programmes.

To explain the baroque styles fully would take several large volumes, and several of these exist.[1] Within the period from 1600 to the middle of the eighteenth century, enormous changes took place, and almost every large musical centre in Europe had its own individual style. This chapter will deal with the general principles common to all geographical areas, with particular reference to central Germany at the time when Bach was composing his Passions. Attention will be drawn to stylistic matters which differ most from those of later times, understanding of which is important if one is to have a true critical appreciation of any baroque work.

In Chapter 1 a brief reference was made to the fundamental changes of style which occurred about 1600 in order to explain how the Oratorio Passion form emerged. Although the old polyphonic style of the sixteenth century (*stile antico*) persisted well into the seventeenth century and in some areas, for example Rome, even into the eighteenth century, the new style (*stile nuovo, stile rappresentativo*) which began in Italy at the turn of the century rapidly spread to all cultural centres in Europe, including those where the old style still remained alive. Many composers wrote in both styles, though not combining the two in one work. The basis of this new music and of baroque composition in general was the replacement of Renaissance contrapuntal strands by the *basso continuo*; or, put another way, the substitution of vertical for horizontal thinking.* The *basso continuo*, being the lowest instrumental voice of a composition, was more or less continuous from beginning to end, even if at times the lowest voice was not in the bass register. The choice of instrument on which the harmonies were played depended on the nature and purpose of the music, the imagination of the composer, and many other factors such as availability of players. The harmonies were indicated by means of figures; the figures gave the intervals above the *basso continuo* of the notes to be played: hence the term 'figured bass'. Omission of the *basso continuo* line was very rare and only for a special symbolic effect; it might for instance go with a situation where the words suggested great anxiety, giving a feeling of there being 'no support'. Bach omitted the continuo in only one and a half movements in his Passions, namely, in the first half of No.33 (Chorus I) and in No.58 in the St Matthew, 'For love my Saviour is dying (Aus Liebe will mein Heiland sterben)', and this gives a wonderful tone picture of Jesus hanging on the cross (above the earth and without its support). The soprano aria in Bach's Cantata No.105 is another superb example of the omission of continuo adding to the feeling of insecurity implied by the words.

It wasn't necessary for any other instruments to be added to the basic solo and bass lines, but before the century was very old other *obbligato*, or *concertante*, instruments were added whose music became an extra melodic line to the two that already existed. With the rapid development of instrumental playing, by the third decade of the seventeenth century several such *concertante* instruments were generally found in a composition, unless it was purely a recitative. So quite early in the seventeenth century the idea of horizontal thinking returned and even when a group of instruments large enough to be called an orchestra was present, in most cases the idea of individual contrapuntal

*There were, however, notable exceptions to this: Schütz stated that he only added a *basso continuo* to his *stile antico* compositions (*Cantiones Sacrae* of 1625—really a mixture of the old and new styles, and *Geistliche Chormusik* of 1648) at the request of his publisher. Furthermore, changes being seldom completely sudden, anticipations of the monodic style can be seen, for example, in certain of Dowland's lute songs before the direct influence of the Italian composers of the new style actually reached the British Isles. Even the *basso continuo* and *obbligato* instrumental writing were partly anticipated by the custom of using instruments to double or replace voices in the Venetian motets, as for example in G. Gabrieli's polychoral works of 1597.

lines was strictly preserved and maintained throughout a movement (though this would not stop any instrument occasionally doubling another melodic line). Here is the fundamental difference between the baroque style and the more harmonic style of the late eighteenth century and the nineteenth, when instruments would flit in and out of the texture in order to complete or colour the harmonies, or double certain notes at a different pitch, the number of 'voices' being able to change from chord to chord.

It follows from this that in principle each movement of a baroque piece has its own generally unchangeable mood and orchestration, both of these being inextricably linked by the Doctrine of the Affections. The word 'affections' (Italian *affetti*, German *Affekte*) had a wealth of meaning in the baroque period, covering general emotions such as sadness, anger or joy; feelings of association; and mental states less easily defined. By the late baroque period, most arias or instrumental pieces had come to be governed by a single affection, expressed by a distinctive and dominant musical idea—rhythmic, melodic or harmonic, each of these alone or in combination. In vocal and vocally inspired pieces, this musical 'formula' represented more or less realistically the single word or idea fundamental to the meaning of the whole. Instruments even came to be classified according to the affections they most effectively expressed—horns being thought of as 'pompous', timpani 'heroic', and so on.[2] Royalty was almost invariably suggested by trumpets and timpani, often on their own (plus continuo);* oboes and flutes, although part of the normal *tutti*, when used alone might suggest a pastoral scene (e.g. the flutes in 'Sheep may safely graze' from Cantata No.208). However, it must be emphasized that there was no absolute rigidity in these matters; the oboe and flute sound alone (and strings, come to that) could in a general way help to paint a sad or poignant scene (for example Nos.12 and 58 in Bach's St Matthew or No.63 in St John).

Chromatic harmonies, for example, were a means for the communication of moods of grief, sadness, despair and the like, whether caused by spiritual anguish or the pangs of unhappy love. But chromatic harmony could also enhance the strength of a cheerful passage, especially at a cadence. Both harmonic and

*The use of a single wind instrument (cornett, slide trumpet, horn or whatever) to back up a vocal line in a chorale is a different matter.

rhythmic 'painting' would be used in a broad sense, to depict the general affection of an orchestral piece, concerted chorus or solo, and also to highlight and interpret individual words—especially within the texturally more free context of recitative. For example, no setting of a word like 'fly' in a recitative by Bach was possible without a melismatic flourish of quick notes; similarly it is extremely rare to find an Oratorio Passion of the mid and late seventeenth century in which the crowing of the cock is not set to a melisma (Theile's St Matthew is the only one I know). Allied to this is the ancient practice of setting or reflecting the meaning of words about downward or upward movement with downward or upward moving music. (This will be made abundantly clear in the detailed discussion of Bach's Passion music in Chapters 5 and 6.) Only a step from this was the custom of reflecting the meaning or shape of any key or emotive word in music; indeed, it was one of the chief means of communication between a composer and his audience.

The use of instrumental colour, harmonic colour and characteristic rhythms for descriptive purposes has been the practice of composers ever since the baroque era, of course, and was not unknown before it. But baroque composers used these elements organically; the appropriate rhythmic figures, harmonic and melodic features suffused the whole substance of a piece.

A proper understanding of the baroque method of word-interpretation through the Doctrine of Affections has been bedevilled by the restricting narrowness of one or two well-meaning writers who have insisted that Bach linked certain musical figures strictly with certain ideas, and have been highly critical of any supposed deviations by Bach from this unnaturally narrow path. Thus, although joy is always expressed by short notes, nearly always including semiquavers, it is misleading to speak of 'the joy motif'. This is because, although the motif in question, of which there are of course an infinite number of variants, does express joy in the right context (e.g. Cantata No.11, last movement), some manifestations of it could just as well express rather different ideas, such as running, laughter, or even a quite different affection (e.g. the upper strings in the St John Passion, No.36). The school of thought that insists on pinning down the meaning of every musical figure to a particular idea in the text is now dying out; but it has caused irrational criticism to be made of

Bach's borrowings from himself, especially in the four short Lutheran Masses,[3] by writers of the last generation. Bach and Handel re-used their own music (and Handel other people's too) as a matter of course, and thought nothing of it; the important thing was that the transfers should be to pieces with the same *basic* affection, though not necessarily to the same precise manifestation of it. Bach's use of the music of the first movement of his Cantata No.46, 'Behold and see if there be any sorrow like unto my sorrow' for the 'Qui tollis' in the Mass in B minor is highly successful, and illustrates the point well. Conversely, the use of a passage from the first movement of Cantata No.102, 'Thou smitest them' for 'Christe eleison (Christ have mercy)' in his G minor Mass is inappropriate and can sound ridiculous in performance.

It may shock some people to be told that Bach was quite willing to have nine movements of the St Matthew Passion adapted to different words by Picander in order to produce memorial music for Prince Leopold of Anhalt-Cöthen at short notice in 1728 when composition of the St Matthew Passion was nearing completion;* moreover these movements include such marvellous pieces as 'Have mercy upon me (Erbarme dich)', No.47 and 'We sit here in tears (Wir setzen uns mit Tränen)', No.78. However, the basic affections of the movements were similar.

*See Chapter 4 for discussion of the relationship of the Funeral Ode to the St Matthew Passion; and see note on page 103 on a recent redating of the first performance of the St Matthew Passion.

3
Performers and Instruments

The instruments which Bach used were all different in sound from those in normal use today; in some cases they were very different. The question might immediately be asked whether therefore we get anything like a true impression of Bach's music when we play it today on modern instruments or, as usually happens, on old instruments which have been modernized. The answer is that we do not; hence the rapidly growing movement for playing it on eighteenth-century instruments or faithful reproductions of them.

In Bach's day all woodwind instruments had far fewer keys than they have today. This must surely have made good intonation and agility harder to achieve than on a modern instrument.

Bach's flute family included several kinds of 'recorders' (*Block-flöten*, usually indicated in the scores as *Flauti*) as well as transverse flutes; the tone of the former is familiar to us, but probably the eighteenth-century instruments were sweeter in tone; certainly the baroque transverse flutes had a far more limpid and soft sound than those of today.

As for the oboe group, it is hard to tell exactly what the tone must have been like because only the finest oboists today attempt to play the old versions of their instruments, and they aim at, and achieve, a refinement of tone that was possibly not expected in Bach's time, but is generally demanded now. From the internal evidence of the music, which implies an even balance between woodwind, string and brass groups, one would guess that the oboe was fairly loud, even allowing that the strings were softer than they are today, since one oboe had to balance two or three violins. That intonation was bad by our standards seems likely; a generation after Bach's death, Charles Burney was complaining bitterly about it.[1] Baroque oboes were of several kinds; oboe, oboe d'amore, an alto instrument mellower in tone than the oboe, and the (curved) oboe da caccia and (straight) taille, both tenor oboes. The bassoon completed Bach's woodwind group; his early works included an instrument whose compass was lower than that of the modern instrument.

Recorders, transverse flutes, oboes d'amore, oboes da caccia and bassoons all figure in the scores of the St John and St Matthew Passions; but bassoons in the latter are included partly by analogy and knowledge of Bach's usual practice; recorders appear only in the St Matthew. The oboe da caccia was associated in the Passions with moments of anguish, both works calling for it in the death scenes or those in close proximity to them. The ordinary oboe was used more in tuttis, but there is a solo in the St Matthew and a duet in the St John. The flute was used extensively in choruses, often doubling the tenor and viola parts an octave higher, as well as solo; in the latter capacity its associations were wide-ranging (compare No.13 in the St John with No.58 in the St Matthew). The use of recorders in No.25 of the St Matthew on the other hand brings out the pathos of the words in a moving manner, especially combined as they are with oboes da caccia.

Since it would have been contrary to the doctrine of the affections to use brass instruments in Passion music, Bach naturally did not write for them in these works.* This brings us to the string family of Bach's time.

The violin, viola and 'cello were less high-powered than they are today, having a lower bridge and being played with a much shorter, lighter and differently shaped bow. In performance this resulted in a softer yet slightly rougher sound, partly because less vibrato was used; but it enabled the player to make an easy separation of notes, which in quick movements brought out the natural dance element which is inherent in most of the music. Vibrato was important as a way of embellishing long notes, that is as an ornament, but was not used as incessantly, nor was it so ferociously wide as it is today. The lowest pitched instrument of the section was the violone. Much has been written in recent years by experts about this instrument, from which it is clear

---

*However, as it was usual in chorale fantasias for a horn to double the choral *cantus firmus* in the soprano part, there seems no reason why it should not double the *ripieno* chorale in No.1 of the St Matthew Passion if it would help to solve balance problems. Indeed, I have done this on more than one occasion.

that the quality of tone, function and pitch varied in different places and at different times during the eighteenth century. From the evidence of the music it is certain that the violone for which Bach wrote in the Passions sounded an octave lower than the 'cello, that is, at the same pitch as the modern double bass. It had a quieter tone, however, and, more important, a more even sound than the double bass as usually played today, lacking the tendency to *fortepiano* which is a characteristic of the modern instrument except when played by an exceptionally sensitive musician, but which bedevils good phrasing in baroque music. The bass viol, or viola da gamba as it is commonly called, was still in occasional use in Bach's time; both the St John and the St Matthew contain a big solo for it. In the St John it is placed right in the centre of the death scene ('It is finished: Es ist vollbracht') and in the St Matthew just before it, when Jesus is carrying his cross.

Other instruments which were semi-obsolete in Bach's time were the viola d'amore, which had extra 'silent' strings which vibrated in sympathy with those that were played, giving a very sweet sound—a pair of these instruments is scored for in the St John Passion (Nos.31 and 32); and the lute, which occurs in the St John with the violas d'amore in No.31.

One of the finest instrumental solos in any Bach score is given to the violin in the St Matthew. It is the grief-laden aria No.47 which follows immediately after Peter's weeping. Sad situations were not however the only ones for which Bach deemed the violin to be the most suitable solo instrument (cf. Cantatas Nos.57, 132, etc.).

Bach's orchestra in Leipzig was made up of *Stadtpfeifer*, or municipal players, some professional musicians and students. On 23 August, 1730, a little over a year after the first performance of his St Matthew Passion,* Bach prepared his famous Memorandum to the Leipzig Town Council on what he considered was necessary 'for a well-appointed Church Music'. In it he set out the minimum and the ideal numbers of both singers and instrumentalists needed for adequate performance of the church music of the day and 'to satisfy the present musical taste'.[2] He complained bitterly about unfilled gaps in the orchestra (some eleven places out of twenty) and the withdrawal of the payments

*But see note on page 103 on a recent redating of the first performance of the St Matthew Passion.

that used to be made in the times of his predecessors to university students who were brought in to fill the gaps. In regard to the regular players who did play for him, Bach made the adverse comment quoted at the end of Chapter 1. The numbers which he considered ideal for ordinary purposes were as follows: two or three first violins, two or three second violins, four violas, two 'cellos, one violone, two or three oboes, one or two bassoons, three trumpets, kettledrums and two flutes if required. In the Memorandum Bach also set sixteen as the ideal number of singers in a choir, that is four to a part; twelve, or three to a part, being the absolute minimum. The Memorandum further stated that there should be a minimum of four 'concertists' (soloists) in each choir, 'sometimes even five, six, seven and even eight; that is if one wishes to perform music for two choirs'.[3]

For the St Matthew Passion as first performed by Bach in 1729* there were probably thirty instrumentalists, seventeen in the first orchestra and thirteen in the second, the choir numbering about forty, that is three or four to a part plus six to eight *ripieno* singers for the chorale in No.1 and possibly No.35.[4] Soloists were the 'concertists' in the choir. The augmentation for this performance would have come from university students.

Bach's choirs were drawn from the fifty-five resident students of the Thomasschule where Bach taught as part of his duties as Cantor. He had to provide competent choirs for three of the Leipzig churches, and chorale singers, that is singers who needed no musical knowledge, for a fourth. So to satisfy Bach's minimum requirements thirty-six capable singers were necessary. Bach's chief complaint in his Memorandum was about the poor musical quality of the students being admitted to the Thomasschule. The effect of this laxity was that much training was necessary for the less experienced and capable singers before they could be useful for the most elaborate music, while some would never be adequate because of their lack of musicality, and he was left in 1730 with only seventeen singers who were 'usable'.[5] The Council made no response to the Memorandum, but a new rector of the school, who appreciated Bach's genius, was appointed the following month, and two years later he managed to get the Council's ruling not to pay for extra orchestral help withdrawn.

Bach was eminently practical, and it is hard to believe that he

*See note on page 17.

would have written so many of his cantatas during his first two
or three years in Leipzig (i.e. c.1724–26) if there had been little
chance of their securing reasonable performances. But we know
that choir discipline deteriorated during his cantorship and with
it would have gone musical standards. In short, one can only
assume that the standard of singing which Bach had for his first
performance of the St Matthew Passion was nothing like the
standard we enjoy today, especially as his Memorandum on
standards was written only seventeen months afterwards.

It is significant that after 1726 Bach composed very few church
cantatas or any sacred vocal works, other than the St Matthew
Passion, the Christmas Oratorio, largely adapted from secular
works, and the Mass in B minor, much of which was adapted
from earlier music. The assumption has been made from this by
some scholars that Bach was disillusioned about the conditions
at the Thomasschule and also about the Church in general. In
fact in 1730 he made great efforts to secure another appointment
in Danzig.

The tone of Bach's choirs must have differed from that of
choirs in Britain and America today, resembling neither non-
vibrato 'white' tone on the one hand, nor operatic tone, with a
wide vibrato, on the other.[6] The best solo singers of the period
probably sang with a small, controlled vibrato, of intensity rather
than of pitch, and with diction which was 'inseparable from the
production of the notes'.[6] This would have given the Passions
and Cantatas the true impassioned operatic interpretation which
they demand. It is extremely unlikely that the students trained
by Bach at St Thomas's ever got very near this standard, but one
can be sure that their tone did not have and did not aim to have
the 'white' pureness of the traditional English choirboy as heard
at the present time, for example, in King's College Chapel,
Cambridge. It is more likely to have been an approximation
between the full-throated sound of the Wandsworth (London)
School boys and the resonant 'continental' sound of the Westminster Cathedral choristers.

This chapter may fittingly conclude with two quotations. If
standards some forty years later are anything to go by, we may
take note of Charles Burney's comment of 1773 that the singers
in Leipzig produced 'just the same pert snap in taking high notes
as in our common singing in England... which they do with a

kind of beat and very loud, instead of a mezza di voce or swell'.[7] And the modern scholar Karl Geiringer arrives at the tragic conclusion that Bach's complicated works, wrought with deepest symbolic meaning, 'were presented in student performances of mediocre quality.'[8]

4
The Texts of Bach's Passions

The texts of Bach's Passions fall into three categories: (1) Bible narrative, (2) interpolated chorales, (3) interpolated free-text choruses, arias, ariosos and recitatives.

Bible narrative

According to his second son, Carl Philipp Emanuel, and the organist-composer L.J.F. Agricola, his student for three years, Bach set the Passion story five times; today, however, we have only the music of the St John and St Matthew complete, and some of the music of a St Mark Passion (1731).[1] It may help to see the two complete works in proportion if it is appreciated that Bach did not pour his whole feelings about the Passion into them, and with this in mind we may briefly examine the St Mark.

The score has been lost, but the text is preserved. There is no extant original score, nor even a copy of it, but many eminent scholars, including Wilhelm Rust, Arnold Schering and Friedrich Smend, have produced strong evidence to support a theory that Cantatas Nos.54 and 198 contain some of the music.[2] If this is correct, and what is missing was on the same level, a work of the highest order has been lost, for these cantatas are among the finest of Bach's compositions. A reconstruction of this Passion was published in 1964,[3] and the first performance in England was given at the Oxford Bach Festival in July 1965 by the London Bach Society[4] directed by Wolfgang Gönnenwein. Cantata No.198, which provides material for the bulk of the reconstruction, is the Funeral Ode 'Lass, Fürstin, lass noch einen Strahl', composed for Queen Eberhardine of Poland, a great benefactress of music. A large orchestra is called for, including two gambas and two lutes; the reason for lutes was to reinforce the continuo which, in this technically 'secular' work, would have been played on a harpsichord. They would not have been necessary in this capacity with the organ continuo used in a Passion performance. The details of the adaptation of most of this work a few years later (1731) and of the first movement of Cantata No.54 are shown in Schmieder's Thematic Catalogue[5] and, of course, in the reconstruction mentioned above.

The text consists of Bible narr. ive (Luther's translation of the New Testament), sixteen chorales, and six arias by Picander, Bach's chief librettist of the time. This is a high proportion of chorales compared with the St John Passion's twelve and the St Matthew's fourteen. A striking difference from the other two Passions in the arias is that two of them are inserted into the Garden of Gethsemane scene immediately after the arrival of Judas and after he has kissed Jesus respectively. The first is: 'He comes, he comes, he is at hand! my Jesu, ah, he seeks thee (Er kommt, er kommt, er ist vorhanden! Mein Jesu, ach, er suchet dich'), and the second: 'False world, thy fawning kisses are poison to faithful souls (Falsche Welt, dein schmeichelnd Küssen ist der frommen Seelen Gift').

It is interesting to compare the two texts in the opening and closing movements of this Passion (they also open and close the Funeral Ode). In Cantata No.198 the words of the first movement begin 'Princess, let yet one ray from Salem's star-vaults shoot, and see, with how many floods of tears we surround thy memorial'. The corresponding movement in the St Mark Passion has 'Jesu, go to thy suffering, I will weep long over thee'. In the last movement the words of the Funeral Ode are 'Yet, Queen, thou diest not, one knows what one has possessed in thee', while the closing Passion chorus is 'In thy grave and gravestone I will always rejoice, Oh Jesu'. From these examples it is plain that the ideas of each movement are similar; in the first, weeping, and in the last, happiness (at the thought of the good life which the deceased led). Certainly the outer movements are as moving in their setting of the texts as are the corresponding ones in the St John and St Matthew, the other sections rather less so. Any attempt at further assessment of the work is difficult and would not be of very much value seeing that none of the music of the biblical narrative exists, and the wedding of music to the chorale words in the reconstruction, although very effective and expressive, is, if anything, more conjectural than what has been done in the case of the choruses and arias. C.S. Terry suggests that in 1731 Bach's relations with the Leipzig Town Council and church authorities were such that he would have felt in no mood to compose a large-scale new Passion; hence his use of earlier material for the music.[6]

St Matthew's account constitutes the longest text of Bach's three extant Passions; the emotions engendered by thoughts about the Passion events run higher here than in St John, which stresses the dramatic elements and, in particular, the long argument between Pilate and the Jews as to whether or not Jesus should be condemned to death. Bach's music makes the most of these differences and as a result we have two strongly contrasted works. A point to be noted is that in St Matthew's Gospel there is a very long section when no *groups* of people, that is, in musical terms, choruses, are involved. This section runs from the disciples' chorus 'Lord, is it I?', Chapter 26, verse 22 to 'He is guilty of death', in verse 66 of the same chapter, a passage of 44 verses. By comparison, the longest gap between choruses of this nature in St John is 18 verses. This long sequence without chorus (*turba*) numbers in the St Matthew Passion possibly accounts for the much greater number of interpolations in that work than in the St John, for these provide variety of texture and colour.

St John's Gospel omits the scene where Jesus's feet are anointed, the last supper and its preparation, most of the Gethsemane scene, Peter's weeping, and the earthquake; but in his setting of St John Bach borrowed two passages from St Matthew, one to heighten the emotion of an already emotional situation, namely the account of Peter's weeping, and one to underline a dramatic one, namely the description of the rending of the veil of the temple, the earthquake, and the saints rising from their graves immediately after Jesus's death. Incidentally, this last scene provided an opportunity to introduce a 'free' commentary on these events. Perhaps Bach chose St John's version for his first Leipzig Passion composition in 1724 because it was short and his time was limited because of the pressure of composing cantatas. Some commentators have in fact suggested that this work was written hastily, citing the repetition of some music in it to different words as a reason.[7] This may indeed be partly true, but, as will be seen in the following chapter, Bach may well have done this because it caused the work to have symmetry of a kind that was evidently very pleasing to him. However, such statements of cause and effect as these must be regarded as conjectural.

Chorales[8]

The first book of chorales, that is, German hymns in the vernacular, was published in 1524, under the title of 'Little Book of Spiritual Songs' (*Geistliches Gesangbüchlein*); it consisted of arrangements of familiar plainsong melodies, secular songs and original compositions, and contained thirty-two hymns and forty-two (mostly five-part) musical settings.[9] This collection sparked off a series of hymn publications, whose melodies were sometimes issued with them and sometimes acquired over the years from independently published books of melodies or melodies with verses. The number of publications increased in size and frequency during the following two centuries until, by 1786, 'an incomplete hymnological index of first lines revealed actually 72,733 German hymns!'[10]

Chorales were the cornerstone of Lutheran worship, and their appearance at focal points in the Passions provided a link between elaborately composed music and that understood and participated in by the people.

A study of the origins of words and music of the chorales Bach used in the Passions shows that he restricted himself not only to those that were associated with Passiontide or death, but also to those that were well known; it is interesting that many of them—both words and music—were published in or near Leipzig.

The placing of chorales in Passions was to some extent traditional. For example, 'Wenn ich einmal soll scheiden (When I come to die)' immediately after the death of Jesus (No.72 in Bach's St Matthew) had for some years been fairly customary (cf. Keiser's St Mark Passion of c.1717), while the sixteenth-century Jakob Handl's 'Ecce, quomodo moritur justus (Behold the righteous man perisheth)', normally sung at the end of the Passion in Leipzig in the eighteenth century, had been traditional in Passions at this point during the greater part of the seventeenth century.[11]

By the time Bach came to use them in his Passions and Cantatas, the chorale melodies had undergone great changes in regard to shape and rhythm since they were first published. The original lively Renaissance rhythms and metrical changes with which most of the melodies in the early hymnbooks were imbued gradually became ironed out, until rhythmically they resembled the four-square 'singable' church hymns of our own day. This was of course in the interests of congregational participation, but it also made the chorales suitable for use in worship in the homes of the devout, for which purpose many simple hymns were also specially composed. From the middle of the seventeenth century onwards, the movement towards personal piety was very strong. To judge from Passion and cantata compositions in the early eighteenth century, only the simplified versions of chorales were in current use in North and Central Germany. Every composer of note left his mark upon them. Some used the very simplest versions, for example, Telemann in his Passions and Handel (with one exception) in his Brockes setting. Others, more immersed in the chorale tradition than Telemann or Handel, naturally gave the chorales treatment which varied suitably according to the context and their own approach to the subject. For example, Keiser who, although he spent his working life in the Hamburg Opera House, was brought up at St Thomas's, Leipzig, in No.5 of his St Mark Passion, which Bach knew, uses the tune and words 'Was mein Gott will' in a version differing little from Bach's in his St Matthew No.31; but he introduces the first line with sopranos only and gives the first note of each phrase two beats. The latter feature might have been incorporated to help the congregation to get started (cf. the old-fashioned 'gathering notes' common in earlier times), but other internal factors suggest that Keiser was not very interested in congregational singing, or that it was not common in Hamburg at the time. By contrast, in No.23 of the same work Keiser sets the same chorale verse, 'O hilf Christe (Help us O Christ)' as Bach does in No.65 of the St John Passion, using the associated tune and an orchestral accompaniment which doubles the voices as in Bach; moreover the expressive character of the harmony is similar to Bach's, and certainly of equal quality. Keiser introduces this chorale after the second 'Crucify' chorus; Bach places it after Jesus's death and the supernatural events that follow it. All of which simply goes to show that plenty of freedom existed in the placing and treatment of chorales.

This brings us to the crucial element in Bach's choral treatment of chorales, which is his harmony and, equally, his presentation of it in terms of vocal euphony. Put another way, the effectiveness of the distribution of notes among the four voices with regard to resonance, timbre, balance and so on, is almost as important as the choice of harmony itself. Many contemporary composers and present-day imitators on courses in academic harmony write strong harmonic progressions on similar principles to those which Bach used, but they seldom come to life because the vocal scoring is dull. Bach's chorale settings for chorus are convincing because he thought through the strongest imaginable harmonic progressions in a linear manner, always bearing in mind the effect of different vocal registers. (In view of this it is a pity that Bach allowed structural considerations to override effectiveness of vocal scoring in so many of his big *ritornello* choruses: compare, for example, bars 119–23 with bars 65–69 in the first Kyrie of the Mass in B minor.) Bach's harmony in his chorale settings is fundamentally based on the most powerful progression in tonal music, namely, from dominant (fifth degree of the scale) to tonic (first degree). It is probably true to say that the basis of at least three-quarters of Bach's chorale harmonizations (and indeed of most of his other compositions) derives from this progression, that is to say they are based on the movement of chords whose fundamental notes stand in the same numerical relationship as dominant to tonic, for example, second to fifth degree, sixth to second and so on. (See Ex.1.) Furthermore, this harmonic movement and all embellishing chromatic notes, and in fact every factor, work with single-minded purpose towards establishing the cadence coming at the end of the phrase as convincingly as possible. The pitch of the various resting points, or cadences, is varied so that the chorale has tonal shape and avoids monotony. All this, including of course the actual selection of notes within the basic progressions explained above—whether plain or chromatic, stolid or using passing notes—is controlled by the need to express the meaning of the words through harmony. Yet, having said this, one has to confess that when two different stanzas are set to the same music, the latter is not always and indeed is very unlikely to be equally suitable to both of them. This point is

Ex. 1: St John No. 15

$$I \quad IV \quad VII^6 \quad I \qquad IV \qquad III^{\#} \ VI \qquad I \qquad V \quad I \qquad V^9 \quad I$$
$$[=V]$$

Temporary key:
C♯ minor

This Chorale (St John No. 15) is a good illustration of the harmonic principles on which Bach worked. Progressions on the V–I pattern are marked ⌐___⌐. The asterisked progression is in effect on the same principle, being IV (= II in function)–V in F sharp minor

further explored in the detailed discussion of Chapters 5 and 6, where further consideration is also given to Bach's expressiveness in his chorale settings.

Among the most famous hymn-writers upon whom Bach drew in his Passions were Johann Heermann (d.1647), author of the Passiontide hymn 'O head full of blood and wounds (O Haupt voll Blut...)' and Johann Rist (d.1667), author of 'Be happy, my soul (Werde munter, mein Gemüthe)'. They wrote poetry of a high standard during the Thirty Years' War which ravaged Central Germany in the first half of the seventeenth century. Naturally, many of their hymns look forward to the joys of heaven as a much longed-for escape from the miseries of the world. In the chorales Bach chose for his Passions the effect of this is seen in the stress placed on the significance of Jesus's death as the means of salvation; see, for example, St John No.27 (Heermann), St Matthew Nos.21 (Gerhardt) and 48 (Rist). The emphasis placed on Jesus as the personal Saviour of man from his sins increased as time went on and was also reflected in the hymns. It was an essential part of Pietism.

In Chapter 1 mention was made of the extreme form of Pietism practised in Halle, of the theologian A.H. Francke's 'mysticism of ardent pain and ecstasy',[12] and of the interpenetration of the language of Pietism between both its adherents and its opponents. That Francke disputed with Thomasius in Leipzig is highly relevant to Bach and his librettists. Blume points out that even the opponents of Pietism like Neumeister (responsible for some of Bach's Cantata texts) 'spoke in a language of mystical, sentimental exaltation or sober reason differing in no way from that of Francke',[13] and that a poet of the calibre of Paul Gerhardt could combine 'the rapturous subjectivity of pietistic devotion with traditional dogma'.[14]

The above may explain the thought behind some chorale texts in the Passions, and specifically, how those most extreme in personalized sentiment came to be written. It may also shed light on the background to some of the 'free' texts.

In the Appendix is a complete list of chorales in Bach's Passions with the authors of the words and the composers of the melodies, when known. It will be seen that both words and music always originated before Bach's time, and in many cases long before it. Apart from making the musical-poetic traditions clear, the list may also serve as a useful reference. The first line of the original version of the melody followed by Bach's version is given in some cases to illustrate the extent to which Renaissance rhythms and outlines became flattened out by the end of the seventeenth and beginning of the eighteenth centuries.

Free texts

For the texts of the arias in his St John Passion, Bach seems to have had some difficulty in finding the ideal collaborator. He drew mainly on two Hamburg poets, and he himself probably made considerable adaptations of their work. A few years earlier a new style of Passion libretto had become fashionable in Hamburg; its essence was the rhymed versification of the Bible narrative and the addition of a large number of reflective arias and recitatives whose sentiments dwelt on the more morbid aspects of the Passion, namely Jesus's physical suffering and the torments of affliction which the Christian believer would feel in contemplating them. Bach's chief source for the St John was *Der für die Sünden der Welt gemarterte und sterbende Jesus* ('Jesus tortured and dying for the sins of the World') by Barthold Heinrich Brockes. Brockes was a Hamburg councillor and amateur poet who became famous through this Passion libretto, published in 1712. The reasons for Brockes's success were that while keeping the style and general flavour of the new Passion libretti, he avoided the most vulgar of the sentiments in which earlier settings had indulged, introduced simple chorales at strategic points, and gave his work an overall structure which lent itself well to musical settings. It quickly became the most popular of the Passion Oratorio texts and was set by the most famous composers of the day, e.g. Keiser, Telemann and Handel. It was natural therefore for Bach to turn to Brockes, and in so doing keep in line with contemporary trends.

The second poet upon whom Bach drew for his St John Passion free texts was Christian Heinrich Postel, an adaptation of whose St John Passion was set in 1704 probably by George Böhm.[15] This incorporated some chorale verses, although in the 1704 setting these are set as free arias.

The free-text pieces in the St John are Nos.1, 11, 13, 19, 31, 32, 48, 58, 60, 62, 63 and 67. No.1 is partly based on Psalm 8 and partly original. Nos.11 and 48 are almost unaltered Brockes; Nos.31 and 32 are fairly close. In No.13, which Terry regards as written by Bach himself, the sentiments are similar to Brockes; Bach has 'I follow thee. . .'; Brockes has 'Take me with you, here is Peter without a sword'; Peter's actual voice in Brockes, but represented by a Christian follower (soprano soloist) in Bach. The words of No.19 are based on the first of Christian Weise's five verses entitled 'The Weeping Peter (Der weinende Petrus)' which they follow very closely. In No.58 both Bach and Böhm have an aria using the words 'Es ist vollbracht (It is finished)' immediately following Jesus's speaking them; the former starts with them and develops ideas from them, the latter uses them as a climactic final line, almost like a refrain. In No.60 the soloist asks the dead Jesus if, because he has been crucified, he (the singer) will be freed from death and Jesus bows his head to say 'Yes', all of which stretches the imagination a good deal; in Brockes, the Daughter of Zion asks Jesus (still living) if her soul's deep wounds are now united with his and she is freed from suffering and death; then a Believing Soul addresses her, saying 'Askest thou this?' And 'For pain Jesus cannot answer, so he bows his head to indicate "Yes"'. Except for one verb and a preposition the words are identical with those set by Bach. This scene is probably the most fanciful one of those inspired by Brockes. No.32, 'Behold, his blood-stained back', represents what seems to us today perhaps the most nauseating expression of thoughts which in themselves are not only perfectly sound, but, as Geiringer believes in regard to No.32 and the preceding arioso No.31, 'reveal, with an intensity rarely equalled in Bach's works, the composer's innermost faith.'[16] Although No.67 expresses thoughts that were traditional in closing Passion choruses and is therefore similar to Brockes, only in the first line are the words the same.

Picander provided all the poems for the St Matthew, and he published them in the second part of his *Ernst-Schertzhaffte und Satyrische Gedichte* in 1729. The fact that these were published separately, that is, not with the biblical narrative and chorales, may indicate that Bach himself selected the latter and indeed may have influenced the writings of his librettist. Picander, whose real name was Friedrich Henrici, was an amateur poet with whom Bach established an increasingly close relationship over the years. Very many of his later choral works both sacred and secular have texts by Picander. He was not only a friend, but also an ally, for in 1729 he collaborated with Bach in the 'Satyric' Cantata (No.201) *Phoebus and Pan* which set out to answer criticisms of Bach's complicated style of composition made by the Leipzig journalist-musician Adolf Scheibe (see Chapter 8). As will be discussed more fully in Chapters 5 and 6, Picander managed usually to express the religious ideas with which Bach was in sympathy in colourful yet restrained language. Certainly the free recitatives and arias in St Matthew are of a high order and contribute in no small measure to the sublime nature of the work.

In contrast to St John's single aria in *Da Capo* form, most arias in the St Matthew have this three-sectional structure. Further comment on the content of the St Matthew lyrics is deferred until Chapter 6, as all the free texts seem to be specially written, except for that of the chorus of No.36 which is from the Song of Songs, VI:1, and for some allusions to poems by Salomo Franck,[17] one of Bach's earlier librettists, in Nos.9 and 74.

5
The Music of the St John Passion

Before discussing the music of Bach's Passions in detail it will be useful to consider his attitude to church music in general. All his life he pursued an ideal and generally seized upon any music, past or present, that could improve his own knowledge or serve as an inspiring model for his own compositions. He excused his absence without leave from Arnstadt with 'I was at Lübeck in order to gain understanding there of one problem and another connected with my art.' But German church music was in a confused state; the choral library of the Michaelkirche at Lüneburg, where Bach spent two and a half years from 1700 singing in the famous Mettenchor, and in his spare time studying, was a hotchpotch of pieces from many periods, following no clear pattern of styles. But Bach supplemented his studies by going to Hamburg to hear the seventy-eight-year-old Reinken, organist at the Katharinekirche and famous for his virtuosity and improvization; he also went to Celle to study the French style (Celle's court was a miniature version of Versailles), and to Lübeck to hear Buxtehude's cantatas and to absorb his ideas as put into practice in the Abendmusik concerts (annual concerts of church music for voices, orchestra and organ which took place in the Marienkirche on the five Sundays before Christmas, following the afternoon service). As early as 1708, when he was only 23, he left Mühlhausen; the reasons he gave for resigning the appointment of organist of the Blasiuskirche ran as follows:

Although it was my intention to advance the music in the Divine Service towards its very end and purpose, a regulated Church music in honour of God, although it was also my intention here to improve the Church music, which in nearly all villages is on the increase and is often better treated than here; although for the purpose of improvement I provided, not without expense, a good supply of the best selected Church compositions, and also in observation of my duty, submitted a project for the repair of the unsatisfactory and damaged organ, and, in short, would have fulfilled my obligations with enthusiasm; it so happened that none of this was possible without vexatious relations... so God willed to bring about an opportunity that will not only put me in a better position so far as the subsistence of my livelihood is concerned, but will also make it possible for me without annoyance, to persevere in working for my very end which consists in organizing Church music well.[1]

Twenty-two years later Bach was still striving to achieve his ideal when he submitted the memorandum in 1730 about the state of the choir and orchestra at the Thomaskirche to the Leipzig Town Council (see Chapter 3). Whether after this it was frustration that caused him more or less to give up composing church music is a matter of conjecture, but his idealism seems never to have abated. Towards the end of his life he compiled three monumental works, solely because he wished to create the best examples he could of works cast in certain forms. These were the Mass in B minor, the *Art of Fugue* and the *Musical Offering*. One may infer from at least the first of these great works that Bach's idealism still produced music of powerful spiritual dimensions. That Bach did broadly share the views of the Church of his time is supported, but not necessarily proved, by the large number of theological books in his private library.

The content of much of the free texts, like some of the chorales, in Bach's Passions and Cantatas, derives from Pietism (see Chapters 1 and 4), their place in the Liturgy from Lutheran Orthodoxy. The Passions came before the sermon (Part 1) and after the sermon (Part II) on Good Friday. Bach first performed his St John Passion in 1724, and the St Matthew in 1729;* he is known to have given three subsequent performances of the St John, and two of the St Matthew.

For his first Passion in Leipzig Bach wrote for a normal-sized Passion orchestra, that is to say two flutes, two oboes, bassoon, strings and continuo; two oboes d'amore and two oboes da caccia are included, but the number of oboe players never exceeds two at any one time. Four additional semi-obsolete instruments are also needed, namely a viola da gamba, a lute and two viole d'amore. Bach scored for a choir consisting of the normal four

*Possibly 1727—see note on page 103.

parts, out of whom six 'concertists' (soloists) were drawn. The function of four of these, namely, a soprano, alto, tenor and bass, was to comment on the Gospel story in movements interpolated into it, designed to draw spiritual lessons or express emotions that the Christian would feel. They also sang the parts of minor characters such as Peter, a servant, Pilate and so on. The other two soloists, a tenor and bass, sang the parts of the Evangelist and Jesus respectively.

Bach does not seem to have been very interested in orchestral colour as such in this work. This is surprising in view of his imagination in this area, which is certainly unsurpassed by anyone else before Rameau and Handel, witness the amazing variety of orchestral sounds he created in the course of composing the Cantatas, not to mention the vast number of different orchestral colours that can be heard in the St Matthew—at least fifteen in the accompanied recitatives and arias alone. Thus in the St John Passion there is only one obbligato for oboes and one for flutes alone; to compensate for this we hear the unique sound of the viole d'amore, once with continuo only and once with a lute, and one gamba solo. The sound of the oboe d'amore is not exploited, but merely employed to cope with the notes below the compass of the normal oboe. The oboes da caccia figure with flutes in No.62 and with solo flute in No.63. But these seven pieces out of a total of sixty-eight provide the only variation from tuttis or near tuttis, strings or continuo only. Bach was more interested in heightening the intensely dramatic nature of the work through the use of tortuous melodies and chromatic harmonies, often highly disturbing in their effect.

St John's narrative of the Passion story does not divide into two parts as satisfactorily as other Gospels do, especially the St Matthew. To divide it more or less equally would have meant splitting down the centre the quick exchanges between Pilate and the mob in Part II; it would also have thrown out of gear a structural plan which was probably thought out by Bach and not just incidental. The symmetry of works like Cantata No.4, *Christ lag in Todesbanden*, or of the motet *Jesu, meine Freude*, affords such positive proof of Bach's interest in palindromic forms (i.e. those that can be read forwards or backwards) that a manifestation of it in the order of movements in the St John Passion cannot be ignored, even if its organization is not precise. In

Cantata No.4, after a brief opening Sinfonia, the seven verses of the chorale on which the work is based are arranged as follows:

1. Chorus.   2. Duet.   3. Solo.
4. *CHORUS.*
5. Solo.   6. Duet.   7. Chorus (Chorale).

Jesu, meine Freude is longer and chorale texts alternate with passages from the Epistle to the Romans. This is the arrangement of movements:

1. 4-part *Chorale.*   2. 5-part Chorus (Romans).   3. 5-part *Chorale.*   4. Trio (Romans).   5. 5-part *Chorale.*
6. 5-part *CHORUS* (Romans).
7. 4-part *Chorale.*   8. Trio (Romans).   9. 4-part *Chorale.*
10. 5-part Chorus.   11. 4-part *Chorale.*

The music of No.1 is identical with that of No.11; No.10 is a shortened version of the music of No.2.

The palindromic plan in the St John Passion from Nos 27 to 52 of course offers one explanation of why Bach used the same music several times. It is not quite so precise in form as in the two works mentioned above. But if one omits the interspersed Evangelist recitatives, and regards Nos.31 and 32 as parallel interpolations with No.48 into a two-unit group, the following diagram emerges, which shows a sufficiently clear retrogressive plan for there to be little doubt that Bach intended it so. Brackets connect the numbers which are nearly or very nearly the same:

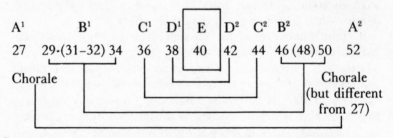

The validity of these transfers is discussed in Chapter 5.

It will be seen from the above examples that a love of symmetry was deeply ingrained in Bach, although it was not typical of other composers of his time. This characteristic links him with composers of the fifteenth and early sixteenth (and twentieth) centuries, and could be one reason why his contemporaries and immediately succeeding generations found him old-fashioned, and why, conversely, his music appeals so strongly to certain academic tastes in the second half of the twentieth century.

The division between Parts I and II of the St John Passion comes after Jesus's seizure and immediately following Peter's denial, but before the trial proper begins. Part I therefore tends to be dramatically static as compared with Part II. Bach makes it more so by what seems a strange insensitiveness, as is explained below. There is a big difference in the number and nature of the interpolations into the Gospel text between this Passion and the later one. Whereas the St Matthew contains 38 interpolations in a total of 78 numbers, the St John has only 14 in a total of 68; St Matthew has 11 accompanied recitatives of a reflective nature, St John only two similar numbers, here called 'ariosos.' But despite the smaller proportion of interruptions to the narration in the earlier work, they are less satisfactorily placed. For example Bach allowed himself to inject two long and beautiful pieces (Nos.11 and 13) into the beginning of the scene in the house of Annas. They are separated by the single phrase (No.12) 'And Simon Peter followed Jesus, and so did another disciple.' So the total interruption time of the narration of important events is considerable. Apart from the interpolations, there are the opening and closing choruses, although the closing one is not in fact the end of the work as, by tradition, one would expect it to be, but is followed by a chorale. Another rather unusual break with tradition is the omission of strings as an accompaniment to the words of Jesus, whose part, like that of the Evangelist, is accompanied only by continuo instruments.

A good deal of emphasis is put on the pictorial element in the discussion that follows, for the illumination of the Word (Bible or hymn verse) in music was not only a technique of Bach's day, but in a special way formed an important part of Bach's purpose in working for a 'regulated Church music', as it did in the case of Schütz about a hundred years earlier. That the wrong kind of emphasis on this aspect can be misleading, however, cannot be too often stressed.

A further matter which carries the danger of overinterpretation is that of tonality. The broad tonal analyses given in this and the next chapter are offered to the reader rather for the sake of

completeness than by way of encouragement to draw any particular conclusions from them. Certainly there are arguments in
favour of associating certain keys with certain moods ('affections'),
eg. E minor with sadness, but it would be unwise to form any
dogmatic opinions in this field. Mattheson, for example, writing
in 1713, referred to the key of E minor as 'sad and pensive', and
such comments by this writer are cited from time to time as if
they had relevance to Bach, his contemporary. But it is uncertain,
in fact unlikely, that Bach knew of Mattheson or of the musical
world on which he immediately based his opinions, when he
composed, for instance, his motet *Jesu, meine Freude* or his
jubilant early Easter Cantata *Christ lag in Todesbanden*, both
in E minor.

Tonal schemes in eighteenth-century works were often influenced by the limitations of trumpets and horns. Thus Bach's
Magnificat, which includes trumpets, begins and ends in D
major, none of its movements is in an unrelated key, and there
are no *secco* recitatives in which wide-ranging modulations could
occur. All the six Cantatas which make up Bach's *Christmas
Oratorio* begin and end in the same key; moreover, the first and
last of them are both in D major. Handel's oratorio *Samson*,
using trumpets, begins and ends in D; his oratorio *Saul*, also
using trumpets, begins and ends in C, and moreover uses this
key at strategic points throughout the work, almost like pillars
to uphold the structure. However, *Messiah* starts in E minor
(without trumpets) and finishes in D (with trumpets).

The tonal schemes of Bach's Passions are not governed by the
fact that trumpets and horns could not play melodic music in any
key at any pitch. The variety of tonal centres used is very
great—not unexpectedly, in view of the imaginatively daring
character of Bach's harmony in other works. The most far-
reaching 'modulations' occur in the *secco* recitatives, and some
accompanied recitatives also begin and end in different keys. (But
one must take a very broad view about such tonal changes in the
light of modern thinking in regard to 'changes of key' in tonal
movements—cf. Schenker's theories, which argue that within any
tonal movement there exist only shifts of emphasis and not
changes of tonal centre.[2] The overall tonal schemes of Bach's
Passions do not seem to conform to any special formal patterns,
apart from the St Matthew and St John (but not the St Mark)

following the tradition of flat keys for the final 'rest in the grave' choruses.

Part I of St John begins in G minor and finishes in A major. The numbers of the first scene, in the Garden of Gethsemane, stay mainly in closely related keys, while those of the second, in the High Priest's Palace, go into sharp keys and finish in that area.

Part II begins in A minor and finishes in E flat major. It is mainly in sharp keys up to the focal point, No.40, of the trial scene, but from there it works back gradually to flat keys. The death scene itself (roughly Nos.55-60) is in sharp keys, but from there to the end of the work the keys gradually flatten towards the subdominant, i.e. flatter side, of the C minor and E flat major of the two final movements.

PART I

1.   Chorus, 'Lord our Governor (Herr, unser Herrscher)'; free text; flutes, oboes, bassoon, strings, continuo (= tutti).

This is a large-scale *Da Capo* movement, both sections of which consistently pursue their musical ideas. These consist of almost continuous semiquavers in undulating four-note groups in the upper strings, over long repeated (or pedal) notes in the basso continuo which also, to break up the pedals, takes over the semiquaver figure from time to time. The upper woodwind, flutes doubling oboes, have long notes, mostly held over to create poignant dissonances on the accented pulses. The chorus sings the violins' and violas' music in its opening statement and wherever it is repeated, but is otherwise independent. The choral parts are declamatory, expressive, and in the sudden *piano* on 'and also in the greatest lowliness (und auch in der grössten Niedrigkeit)', realistic. The choral opening is big: 'Lord, our Governor, whose fame in all lands is glorious (Herr, unser Herrscher...)' (cf. Psalm 8). The result should be magnificent, but balance problems between the various groups in modern performances are great and the woodwind parts are seldom audible. It is probably best not to fasten particular interpretations onto the various musical themes in this movement, for the four-note semiquaver groups could have numerous associations in Bach's music (see Chapter 2). Certainly the upper woodwind has sad plaintive music, while the chorus, when doubling the string semiquavers, are dealing with a majestic idea which is associated throughout this movement with the word 'Governor'.

2(2a).*   Recitative, Evangelist and Jesus, 'Jesus went forth with his disciples (Jesus ging mit seinen Jüngern)'; continuo

The story set by Bach from St John, the Gospel for Good Friday, begins with Jesus and the disciples going to the Garden of Gethsemane (not actually named), where immediately Judas appears with a crowd come from the High Priests and Pharisees to arrest him (cf. the St Matthew Passion where the arrest occurs in No.32). The music registers the disturbing effect of Judas's arrival with a sudden chromatic chord (diminished seventh) in bar 5 on 'And Judas also, which betrayed him (Judas aber, der ihn verriet)', and short, jerky phrases on 'with lanterns and torches and weapons (mit Fackeln, Lampen, und mit Waffen)'. Jesus asks them 'Whom seek ye? (Wen suchet ihr?)' The key first word of this question is placed early, that is on, rather than after the cadence of the phrase leading to it, as is normal—Jesus does not keep them waiting wondering what he will do.

3(2b).   Chorus, 'Jesus of Nazareth (Jesum von Nazareth)'; tutti

The crowd answers quickly, vigorously, in short declamatory chords. Flutes doubling first violins have continuous semiquavers rattling out an arpeggio pattern which roughly outlines the soprano part. The basic material of these four bars, especially the flute/violin pattern and the basso continuo, is used in four later movements, Nos.5, 25, 29 and 46; in each case the attitude of the people is similar, that is to say they are Jesus's enemies and demonstrating the fact by what they are saying ('It is not lawful', 25, 'Not this man but Barabbas', 29, 'We have no king but Caesar', 46). Thus the musical transfer largely accords with

*In this and the next Chapter, the numbers in brackets in the itemized discussion are those used in the Neue Bach Ausgabe. First-placed numbers are those of the Bach Gesellschaft edition, and are used in references throughout this book. See Bibliography for full details of these editions.

the Doctrine of Affections (see Chapter 2) and helps to give unity to the work.

4(2c).   Recitative, Evangelist and Jesus, 'Jesus saith unto them (Jesus spricht zu ihnen)'; continuo

At Jesus's reply 'I am he (Ich bin's)' the crowd retreats and falls to the ground instead of coming forward to seize him; see Ex.2, which in some inexplicable way expresses the retreating backward (is it the rising diminished fifth to D flat?) in its first phrase, as well as the more easily depicted falling to the ground in its second phrase.

Ex. 2: St John No. 4

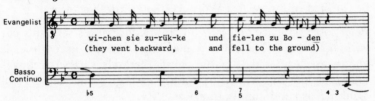

5(2d).   Chorus, 'Jesus of Nazareth (Jesum von Nazareth)'; oboes, strings and continuo

The crowd's answer here is far less confident than in No.3; the music is virtually the same but in a flatter key; the sparkling flute and violin passage of No.3 starts as much as a fifth lower and the flutes are omitted from it. The course of the arrest has been momentarily checked.

6(2e).   Recitative, Evangelist and Jesus, 'Jesus answered: I have told you (Jesus antwortete: Ich hab's euch gesagt)';

Jesus gives himself up but, in seven notes in quasi-arioso style, asks for his disciples to go free.

7(3).   Chorale, 'O mighty love (O grosse Lieb')': tutti

The first interpolated chorale contrasting Jesus's great love and suffering with man's living in the world in joy and pleasure. The personal element is present with the use of 'I' and 'Thou'. The melody is 'Herzliebster Jesu' pitched rather low in G minor. The scoring is expressive and there is lavish use of chromaticism in painting such phrases as 'This way of torment (Diese Marterstrasse)' and 'Thou must suffer (Du musst leiden)'. This chorale melody is also the first one to be interpolated in the St Matthew, but there, to fit the key scheme, it is pitched a major third higher. Yet here the harmonic treatment is more striking. In fact the chorale settings in this work are unsurpassed in either of the other two works which abound in them, namely, the St Matthew Passion and the *Christmas Oratorio*.

8(4).   Recitative, Evangelist and Jesus, 'That the saying might be fulfilled (auf dass das Wort erfüllet würde)'; continuo

Peter loses patience and cuts off the High Priest's servant's ear with his sword. The music's meaning, through its outline, is almost as clear as that of the words themselves. Jesus rebukes him, and 'the cup which my Father hath given me, shall I not drink it?' is sung mainly in arioso style.

9(5).   Chorale, 'Thy will be done, Lord God (Dein Will' gescheh', Herr Gott)'; tutti

The tune of 'Vater unser in Himmelreich (Our Father which art in Heaven)' is set to a stanza of Luther's versification of the Lord's Prayer. The third phrase asks for patience in time of trouble ('Gib uns Geduld in Leidenszeit') and, in the light of Peter's impatience in No.8, may be a reason for this verse being chosen here. The greater tranquility which this chorale possesses as compared with No.7 derives from the large number of perfect cadences in full (or root) position, five out of six; No.7 has two out of five. The smaller number of chromatic notes is also a contributory factor.

10(6).   Recitative, Evangelist, 'Then the band and the captain (Die Schar aber und der Oberhauptmann)'; continuo

The scene in Annas's house begins and, as was mentioned in the discussion of the overall structure of Part I, it is interrupted after a few bars because of the reference to Jesus being 'bound'. The final phrase is notable for its chromatic ('neapolitan') chord on 'die (umbracht)'.

11(7).   Aria, Alto, 'From the snare of my sins (Von den Stricken meiner Sünden); free text; oboes and continuo

Bach casts dramatic considerations to the winds and inserts this beautiful aria about the sins which bind the Christian also binding his Saviour. The main obbligato theme (which the voice only copies and embellishes when it enters) has a down-up-down-up (-down) contour, perhaps the nearest thing that orthodox music can get to describing the binding; the constantly heard continuo figure also alternates down-up movement and includes 'restricting' repeated notes. The two oboe parts seem inextricably intertwined, apparently symbolic in a different, more literal way of the text. There may be significance too in the suspensions, on ties, implying binding or fastening, which are an integral part of the oboes' music (see bars 2–3, 3–4, 4–5, etc).

12(8).   Recitative, Evangelist, 'And Simon Peter followed Jesus (Simon Petrus aber folgete Jesu nach)'; continuo

These three bars linking two big arias have already been mentioned. They contain a clear anticipation of the notes of the melody of the following aria (see Exs.3 and 4).

Ex. 3: St John No. 12

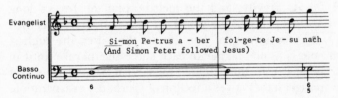

Ex. 4: St John No. 13

13(9).   Aria, Soprano, 'I follow Thee also (Ich folge dir gleich-falls)'; free text; flutes and continuo

It was natural in view of this text for Bach—or any competent composer of his time—to contrive some kind of realism in the music. The beginning of the main tune is treated in canon nearly every time it comes. The canon is between the *basso continuo*, voice and flutes, in that order, but the continuo gives up rather earlier than the others. This reflection of the meaning of the words in the music was one of the aids to understanding that eighteenth-century audiences expected. The aria is the most cheerful piece in the whole work; the impression of running after someone is very clear, and the upward scale movement in the opening bars is, not surprisingly, paralleled in those of No.48 ('Haste'), in fact the first bar of No.13 is identical melodically with the second of No.48. (See Ex.4.)

14(10).   Recitative, Evangelist, Jesus, Peter (Bass), Servant (Tenor), 'That disciple was known unto the High Priest (Der-selbige Jünger war dem Hohenpriester bekannt)'; continuo

Jesus is taken from Annas's house to the High Priest's palace. This movement includes Peter's first denial, Jesus's disdainful answer to the High Priest's questions about his teaching, the High Priest's servant striking Jesus in the face, and Jesus asking for proof that he has spoken evil. Points to be noticed are: Peter's simply declaimed denial (bars 14 and 15) which in No.18 is repeated a tone higher for additional emphasis; the melisma on 'warmed (themselves) (wärmeten sich)' in bar 19 which stands out because it is the only one in the whole movement, and is effective for its brevity; and the melodic plan of Jesus's long speech 'I spake openly to the world... (Ich habe frei, öffentlich geredet...)', beginning at bar 25. In the latter the highest accented note is a tone higher in each successive phrase until in the last bar of it (36) the accented high E on 'what *I* have said (was *ich* gesaget habe)' gives a feeling of (perhaps) exasperation.

15(11).   Chorale, 'Who dares to smite Thee (Wer hat dich so geschlagen)'; tutti

The placing of the voices and high pitch of this chorale—a protest at the injustice of a physical attack on Jesus (14)—make the dissonance in bar 2 most effective. In verse 1 it occurs on 'smite (thee)' ('schlag'- of 'dich so geschlagen'), and on 'sins (Sünden)' in verse 2, in both cases very suitably.* In strophic settings the fact must be faced that some of Bach's 'word-interpretative' chords fit less well in repetition. But in verse 2 the repetition 'I, I and my sins... (Ich, ich und meine Sünden...)' is apt, stressing more emphatically the Christian's personal involvement; this is not Bach's original idea of course, but Paul Gerhardt's, the author of the words, though Bach can have credit for selecting it, or agreeing to its selection. However, this repetition of the pronoun occurs many times in Bach's works, and was traditional (cf. Schütz's St Matthew Passion and Bach's, in No.16 below, words by Paul Gerhardt, or the opening of the first chorus in Cantata No.21, author unknown, but possibly Franck—'I, I, I, I had much affliction'). The latter was criticized by the eighteenth-century Hamburg musician and writer Mattheson who, like most of his contemporaries, regarded Bach as hopelessly old-fashioned.

16(12a). Recitative, Evangelist, 'Now Annas had sent him bound (Und Hannas sandte ihn gebunden)'; continuo

In bar 4 we are again told that Peter warmed himself by the fire (see No.14, bar 21); it is curious, but not apparently significant, that the melisma here on 'warmed (wärmete)' is almost, but not quite, identical with that in No.14, bar 19, which referred to the soldiers and servants, but is here a third lower.

17(12b). Chorus, 'Art not thou also one of his disciples? (Bist du nicht seiner Jünger einer?)'; tutti

The officers and servants tax Peter about his identity in this short chorus, which has a light, open texture, lightened still further by the effect of the staccato marks put in the score by the composer. It consists entirely of two musical ideas. One is a fugato theme (i.e. one that is imitated by other voices), which is announced by the tenors and passed successively to altos, sopranos, back to tenors and on to basses before the tenors have finished, to altos

*See note on page 59.

before the basses have finished, then to sopranos and finally to
basses. The other idea is a quick three-note figure repeating the
first part of the question 'Art not thou (also one of his disciples)?
(Bist du nicht. . . ?)'. The effect is extraordinary: one can
positively hear many voices all talking at once, asking the same
question about Peter's identity with increasing persistence.

18(12c).   Recitative, Evangelist, Peter, Servant, 'He denied it,
and said (Er leugnete aber und sprach)'; continuo

No wonder Peter immediately denies any knowledge of Jesus
with more emphasis (that is, at a higher pitch) than before; the
cold, and those voices coming at him in No.17, must be unnerving
indeed. He suffers yet one more question—this time from a
servant, 'Did not I see thee in the garden with him?' Peter denies
with even more vehemence; but his third denial is only stated by
the Evangelist, not, as in St Matthew's version, actually put into
Peter's mouth. The crowing of the cock is beautifully set here,
a restrained yet effective phrase for the voice and a simple
arpeggio for the continuo; it makes rather more impact than the
later setting does. But in Peter's weeping, not recorded by St
John, but here borrowed from St Matthew, the long melismas
on 'wept (weinete)' are both more and less telling than the
parallel passage in the later work. They are far longer, more
elaborate and poignant in both melody and harmony, but in the
context of the work as a whole, this weakens their impact. Bach
uses melismas for special words only and his normal treatment
is masterly because of its restraint. We have already noticed the
treatment of 'warmed (themselves)' in No.14 and the reasons for
its effectiveness; it is unique in the movement, and of only one
and a half beats' duration. For the Evangelist suddenly to indulge
in *two* long melismas on the same word, each of six beats'
duration, gives the impression of his stepping out of his role as
narrator, although what he is doing is, admittedly, only an
extravagant extension of what is legitimate, and is in itself very
beautiful. The proportions, namely the melismatic emphasis
given to the word vis à vis that given to the words in the rest of
the narration, are far better in the later work, where the real
weeping comes in the following aria. Compare also the treatment
of a much more important event later in the St John—Jesus's

death—in No.59, where a two-note melisma makes a more moving effect.

19(13).   Aria, Tenor, 'Ah, my soul (Ach, mein Sinn)'; free text; strings,* bassoon and continuo

It is Peter's despair rather than his bitter weeping which is depicted in the dotted rhythms and jagged outlines of this tenor aria. In the St Matthew aria, at the corresponding place, his weeping is continued by the alto soloist. The mood being what it is, if ever there were a case for making the rhythm more jerky through dotting by analogy, and tightening the dotted figure by near double dotting, it is here. Some modern forms of notation, e.g. the double dot, had not been invented in Bach's time, and many written rhythms were capable of several interpretations, according to the context. In this aria, bar 33 gives the clue needed not only for the interpretation of bar 35, but also for the whole piece. It is obviously a sequential passage which sounds ludicrous if the answer in bar 35 is sung in a different rhythm from the statement in bar 33 (see Ex.5). Although here it could have been notated accurately, it is a well-known fact that, to save time, composers of Bach's time took short cuts: it was quicker to write a quaver rest and a quaver than to add a semiquaver rest (or dot the quaver rest) and add two tails to the first note of the bar. Should anyone doubt this, one has only to look at the autograph score of the St Matthew Passion for example, and compare the quickly-written long notes of the continuo part of the *secco* recitatives there with the short notes and rests of the original orchestral parts. So by musicological deduction, did not musical considerations cry out for it, the rhythm of the opening theme

Ex. 5: St John No. 19

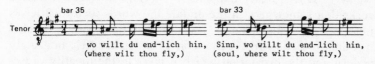

*The indication *Tutti li stromenti* means that other instruments (that is, woodwind) should also participate.

Ex. 6: St John No. 19

must always be played as indicated by the symbols above the staff in Ex.6, and generally tightened.

For the same reason, namely to save time, we find certain ornaments are often missing from baroque scores. This aria again, like its opposite number (No.47) in the St Matthew, becomes much more effective if ornaments are added by analogy, for example bar 17 from bar 1, and so on. The ending, if played strongly, as marked by the composer, maintains the feeling of despair, and has a parallel in the St Matthew's No.36, where the Daughter of Zion(?), having searched in vain for Jesus in the garden, exhibits a similar feeling with a similar cadence.

20(14).   Chorale, 'Peter, unreflecting (Petrus, der nicht denkt zurück)'; tutti

The first four phrases of the chorale summarize what Peter has done; in the last bar of the fourth phrase there are exceptionally expressive-descriptive melismas in alto and tenor on 'weeps (weinet)'. It frequently happens in chorales throughout Bach's works that somewhere in the middle the words turn themselves into a prayer. This one asks Jesus to 'look upon me ... when I have done evil (Böses)'; the chord on 'Böses' in bar 13 is amazingly modern and the disruption which it gives to the tonality causes a slight shock even today. What Bach's audience in 1724 must have thought cannot be imagined.

PART II

21(15). Chorale, 'Christ, who makes us blessed (Christus, der uns selig macht)'; tutti

'Christ, who makes us blessed, no evil has committed (... kein Bös's hat begangen)': the repeated soprano Es at the beginning ring out in such a way as to give this chorale which opens Part II the quality almost of a motto, summarizing the essence of what is to follow. Again, Bach stretches the harmonic resources of his time suitably to colour 'evil (Bös's)' in phrase two and 'thief (Dieb)' in phrase four.

22(16a). Recitative, Evangelist, Pilate (Bass), 'Then led they Jesus from Caiaphas (Da führeten sie Jesum von Caiphas)'; continuo

Jesus is taken to Pilate, who here begins his long argument with the Jews about the question of his guilt. It lasts until No.47. The phrases describing Jesus's journey are jagged, giving the impression of haste and unpleasant conditions (it is in the middle of a cold night); those about the Jews not going inside the judgment hall 'lest they should be defiled' at Passover time are lyrical and smooth. Pilate asks them what complaint they have against Jesus.

23(16b). Chorus, 'If he were not a malefactor (Wäre dieser nicht ein Übeltäter)'; tutti

This disrespectful answer is set to rough music whose structural basis is the rising chromatic scale announced (bars 1–4) in the bass, but 'covered' by the three other voices, so that it has to be listened for. It is melismatically descriptive of 'Übeltäter', and having reached the top, it falls down in a few chromatic but semitonal steps the other side. This up-down theme is always present except in bar 14 and part of 15 and the closing four bars, but other music goes on at the same time. It constantly overlaps itself which adds to the effect.

24(16c).   Recitative, Evangelist, 'Then said Pilate unto them, Take ye him (Da sprach Pilatus zu ihnen: So nehmet ihr ihn hin)'; continuo

Pilate tries to rid himself of Jesus by telling the Jews to judge him by their own, not Roman, law. One wonders if Bach, in giving Pilate virtually identical music to that which he has just sung in No.22, and in following it with a chorus strongly related to No.23, is deliberately emphasizing the repetitive character of the argument which arises from the entrenched positions of the participants.

25(16d).   Chorus, 'It is not lawful for us to put any man to death (Wir dürfen niemand töten)'; tutti

The Jews will have none of Pilate's suggestions. This short chorus uses the main theme of No.23 descriptive of 'Übeltäter', only here it is set to 'töten'; the two words are sufficiently similar in meaning, in that they both suggest evil things, for this transfer to work satisfactorily. The key and treatment of the basic material are different from those of No.23. There is also a link with four other movements, Nos.3, 5, 29 and 46, through the use of the semiquaver figure common to all of them.

26(16e).   Recitative, Evangelist, Jesus, Pilate, 'That the saying of Jesus might be fulfilled (Auf dass erfüllet würde das Wort Jesu)'; continuo

In referring to Jesus's prophecy about his death, Bach highlights 'die (sterben)' in his customary manner by a melisma and chromatic harmony. Pilate now addresses Jesus for the first time, asking him: 'Art thou the King of the Jews?' Jesus delays a direct reply. Although Bach gives Jesus a calm, relaxed phrase—on one chord for six beats—Pilate's annoyance is evident from his snappy answer: 'Am I a Jew? (Bin ich ein Jude?)' in which the harmonies move on much more quickly—three times as quickly at first—than do those given to Jesus. From now on Jesus's answers do not annoy, but totally mystify Pilate, who can have no idea what Jesus means by 'My Kingdom is not of this world (Mein Reich ist nicht von dieser Welt)' (bars 16–17); and Bach's elaborate melisma, even imitated in the continuo, on 'fight (kämp-fen)' in 'then would my servants fight' adds to the enigmatic nature of Jesus's answer by its fanfare-like shape, suggesting a call to battle.

27(17).   Chorale, 'O great King (Ach, grosser König)'; tutti

This setting of the chorale melody 'Herzliebster Jesu' (cf. No.7) is with continuous quavers in the bass which gives it a majestic quality eminently suitable for the opening words of verse 1: 'O great King, great for all time. . .' For the rest of verse 1, and in verse 2, these quavers have to be interpreted differently to make sense. This is a good example of how important it is in general not to tie any musical figure down to a one-only interpretation (see Chapter 2). Even the pictorial passages in the recitatives, or at least most of them, in another context could equally well illustrate other, similar, words. This number is A^1 in the diagram of the palindrome at the beginning of this chapter.

28(18a).   Recitative, Evangelist, Jesus, Pilate, 'Pilate therefore said unto him, Art thou a King then? (Da sprach Pilatus zu ihm: So bist du dennoch ein König?)'; continuo

Jesus explains that his end is to 'bear witness unto the truth'. The emphasis given by Bach to Jesus's explanation, in the high tessitura at cadences, underlines what must be its incomprehensibility to Pilate, who asks the question 'What is truth?', but without waiting for an answer goes out and tells the Jews that he can find no fault in Jesus. Reminding them of the custom of releasing one prisoner at the Passover, Pilate asks if he should release the 'King of the Jews'; a slow harmonic rhythm gives Pilate's words to the Jews a relaxed, unprovocative character.

29(18b).   Chorus, 'Not this man but Barabbas (Nicht diesen sondern Barrabam)'; tutti

The Jews' answer 'Not this man but Barabbas' makes its point by being brief and declamatory; no lengthy contrapuntal elaborations are allowed to hold things up, as they do later in the work (see Nos.38 and 54). The use of the semiquaver theme from No.3 (see also Nos.25 and 46) is yet another illustration of the point referred to under No.27; see also what was said about No.3 for the validity of these transfers, and in Chapter 2. With No.34, this is the first B¹ movement in the diagram of the palindrome at the beginning of this chapter.

30(18c).   Recitative, Evangelist, 'Now Barabbas was a robber (Barrabas aber war ein Mörder)'; continuo

The German construction with 'aber' ('but' or 'now') after the proper noun, Barabbas, enables Bach to write a powerful phrase starting on a very high note, wonderfully interpreting the horror that Christians feel at the Jews' choice of a criminal, instead of Jesus, for release (see Ex.7); that Bach crashes in immediately with this phrase without the usual preliminary chord contributes much to its effect. Pilate has declared Jesus innocent, but has risked his being chosen for punishment and now sees this happen: 'Then Pilate therefore took Jesus, and scourged him (Da nahm Pilatus Jesum und geisselte ihn)'. Bach again allows the Evangelist to paint a horrific picture, by writing a melisma of 49 notes in cruelly realistic rhythms on 'gei-' of 'geisselte (scourged)'. The principle involved here was discussed under No.18 in connection with Peter's weeping. In both cases, the weeping and the scourging, Bach keeps things much more in proportion in the St Matthew Passion by reserving the pictorial aspect for the movement immediately following the Evangelist's statement (see St Matthew Passion, Nos.47 and 60).

Ex. 7: St John No. 30

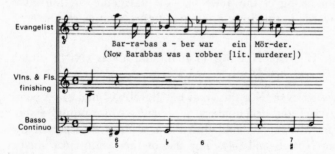

31(19).   Arioso, Bass, 'Consider, my soul (Betrachte, meine Seel')'; free text; two viole d'amore (or two muted violins), lute, bassoon and continuo

The exquisite sound of this arioso arises from its unique instrumentation and the effect of dissonances over repeated bass notes. Nothing like it (apart from the next piece, which lacks the lute) is to be found in any other Bach composition. It is appropriate to say 'is to be found' rather than 'Bach never wrote' for we shall probably never know what marvellous music has not come down to us in the hundred or so lost church cantatas. The message of this number is clear, though it may mean different things to different listeners. Geiringer sees it as a 'vision of celestial bliss arising out of physical pain'.[3]

32(20).   Aria, Tenor, 'Behold, how his bloodstained back (Erwäge, wie sein blutgefärbter Rücken)'; free text; two viole d'amore (or two muted violins), and continuo (without violone or bassoon)

The instrumental figures in this long and beautiful aria have been associated by most commentators with the rainbow mentioned in the second half of the text. Yet the motifs concerned are generically the basic baroque figures depicting grief or sighing. Moreover the very long melisma on the word 'rainbow (Regenbogen)' is characterized by its long notes and the use of entirely different melodic shapes from those heard before, and bearing little resemblance to a rainbow. That individual reactions to pictorial music may and should be free has been said already several times. The important thing is to realize that the music of Bach's time, and his in particular, *is* pictorial. If Bach intended to paint a rainbow, many people may find that they hear it more through the tearful colour of the obbligato instruments (seeing a rainbow through rain) than through the actual melody. What is musically striking is the subtle use of 'hemiolic' patterns, or the displacement of accents so that new metres are temporarily felt; these are scattered through the movement, thus preventing the longest piece in either Passion (over nine minutes) from becoming monotonous; see bars 4, 7, 11, 12, 13, 14, 16, 21, 23, 25, 29, 31, 33, 35—and possibly the second half of 39 (possibly, because although the cadence is the normal place to find a hemiola, and the music contains one, the natural accentuation of the word involved, 'Gnadenzeichen (token of favour)', works against it). The music of this piece transcends the text which derives from Brockes (see Chapter 4).

33(21a).   Recitative, Evangelist, 'And the soldiers plaited a crown of thorns (Und die Kriegsknechte flochten eine Krone von Dornen)'; continuo

Four and a half bars of recitative describing Jesus receiving a crown of thorns and purple robe take us into the following chorus. The implied D major harmony of the opening bars may possibly be intended to suggest Jesus's non-resistance to these insults.

34(21b).   Chorus, 'Hail, King of the Jews (Sei gegrüsset, lieber Judenkönig)'; tutti

Literally, 'We greet you, dear King of the Jews', with the sarcastic interpolation of the word 'dear (lieber)'. It is sad that the downward four-note group of semiquavers repeated on woodwind without cessation from the second bar until two beats from the end is smothered in the vocal and string texture, and is almost impossible to hear unless a very small choir and baroque instruments are used, and the flutes and oboes are reinforced by violins, as Bach himself did in his third and fourth performances of the work. These rushing notes sound to this writer like the rapid and mocking bowing of many knees. The choral music, doubled by strings, is a tightly-knit *fugato* with eight entries of the subject; soprano, alto, tenor, bass, tenor, bass, soprano, alto, a few bars of impressive chordal writing, and a final subject entry in the bass. This chorus, with No.29, stands as the second at B^1 in the diagram of the palindrome.

35(21c).   Recitative, Evangelist, Pilate, 'And they smote him with their hands (Und gaben ihm Backenstreiche)'; continuo

Pilate, who at the end of No.30 was responsible for scourging Jesus, now goes out again to the Jews and declares more emphatically, in less simple music than in No.28, that he finds no fault in him: he even brings Jesus out for them to see, wearing the crown of thorns and the purple robe, and in a vividly expressive four-note phrase, the substance of which is only a conventional formula, sings 'Behold the man'. The High Priests and servants are enraged, as the Evangelist's leading-in phrase shows.

36(21d).   Chorus, 'Crucify (him) (Kreuzige)'; tutti

They clamour for his death. Bach builds the music from a double sustained theme in long notes involving dissonances and an upward leap of a fourth, announced immediately by sopranos and altos and a short, quick repeated figure (see Ex.8). These themes are worked out in combination while most of the instruments hammer out the rhythm of Ex.8 without a break from start to finish. The impact on the ear is rough and the texture thick. This chorus is C^1 in the diagram of the palindrome.

Ex. 8: St John No. 36

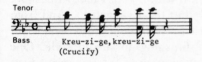

Tenor

Bass   Kreu-zi-ge, kreu-zi-ge
        (Crucify)

The pattern of the later version is:—

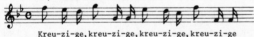

Kreu-zi-ge, kreu-zi-ge, kreu-zi-ge, kreu-zi-ge

37(21e).   Recitative, Evangelist, Pilate, 'Pilate saith unto them, Take ye him (Pilatus sprach zu ihnen: Nehmet ihr ihn hin)'; continuo

Pilate tries to push responsibility for the crucifixion onto the Jews, repeating more emphatically still (shorter notes and phrases, quicker harmonic movement) that he finds Jesus innocent. The Jews then invoke one of their laws.

38(21f).   Chorus, 'We have a law (Wir haben ein Gesetz)'; tutti

They say that by that law Jesus should die because he made himself the Son of God. The movement is worked out musically in a formal fugue of a suitably pompous nature. Dramatically its length makes it weak, thirty-three bars of four beats each. No.34, similar in structure, is exactly half as long and twice as effective, apart from the balance problem. This chorus is D^1 in the diagram of the palindrome.

39(21g). Recitative, Evangelist, Jesus, Pilate, 'When Pilate therefore heard that saying (Da Pilatus das Wort hörete)'; continuo

Pilate, now more frightened than ever, goes back and asks Jesus whence he came. Receiving no answer he makes a further effort to release him, reminding him of his power over him. There is a powerful phrase beginning with an upward scale at 'knowest thou not that I have power to crucify thee (weissest du nicht, dass ich Macht habe, dich zu kreuzigen...)' with a twist on 'crucify (kreuzigen)'. Jesus deflates him with 'Thou couldest have no power at all against me, except it were given thee from above (Du hättest keine Macht...)', interestingly set to music whose beginning is almost identical with that of Pilate's question. The music with which Bach clothes the Evangelist's 'And from thenceforth Pilate sought to release him' contains a wonderful change from minor to major, finishing in arioso style. One wonders if the composer was deliberately trying to express here the feeling that Jesus's release would arouse in the believer.

40(22).   Chorale, 'Through thy imprisonment, O Son of God (Durch dein Gefängnis, Gottes Sohn)'; tutti

Some chorales draw lessons and morals, others comment on a situation, but this one without deviating epitomizes in every phrase the central meaning of the Passion, and so makes the most fitting centre possible of the palindrome. The music of the last phrase hints at remote keys in a daring manner rare even in Bach's works (see Ex.9). (A parallel instance is the famous chorale at the end of Cantata No.60, immortalized in Berg's Violin Concerto, but there the harmonies fall more naturally into a logical tonal scheme.) The object here is to depict the dread of everlasting bondage had not Jesus himself submitted to bondage (see the penultimate phrase). This thought is rather obscurely

Ex. 9: St John No. 40

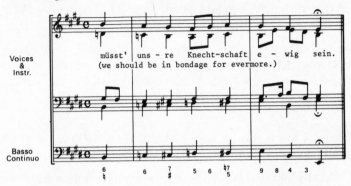

expressed in the text, but as so often happens in Wagner as well
as in Bach, the meaning of the words is clarified by the music.

41(23a).   Recitative, Evangelist, 'But the Jews cried out, saying
(Die Juden aber schrieen und sprachen)'; continuo

One phrase introduces the following chorus.

42(23b).   Chorus, 'If thou let this man go (Lässest du diesen
los)'; tutti

The palindromic structure first becomes apparent here (this is
D²), for the music is identical with No.38, apart from key and
rhythmical alterations. However, the latter are important, particularly in the opening phrase where more notes of shorter value,
necessary to fit the new text, take away the pomposity which was
suited to No.38; here they underline the urgency of 'If thou let
this man go, thou art not Caesar's friend'. The Jews try desper-
ately to get round the barriers of law and fair play which are
delaying the fulfilment of their purpose. The musical transfer
therefore strikes the listener as perfectly acceptable in the opening
phrases, and the wedding of the new words ('whosoever maketh
himself a king speaketh against Caesar') to the music previously
set to 'because he made himself the Son of God' satisfies the
Doctrine of Affections through the regal qualities common—
however inappropriately in Christian terms—to Caesar and the
Son of God.

43(32c).   Recitative, Evangelist, Pilate, 'When Pilate therefore heard that saying, he brought Jesus forth (Da Pilatus das Wort hörete, führete er Jesum heraus)'; continuo

Pilate still does not give in, but provokes the crowd further with 'Behold your King (Sehet, das ist euer König)', but this time to an unconvincing phrase which falls away and lacks the strong, appealing quality of that in No.35 ('Behold the man').

44(23d).   Chorus, 'Away with him, crucify him (Weg, weg mit dem, kreuzige ihn)'; tutti (oboe II is an oboe d'amore)

The 'Crucify' chorus (No.36) is repeated in substance a semitone lower—compare the St Matthew Passion, Nos.54 and 59 where 59 is a tone higher for added emphasis. Three bars of furious shouts of 'Away, away with him (Weg, weg mit dem)' are attached to the beginning of it, and recur later. This is C^2 of the palindrome, and no aesthetic or musicological problems arise in the musical transfer, for the words are similar to those of C^1. The stronger impact of the *four* notes to 'crucify him (kreuzige ihn)' in the final bar as compared to the *three* notes to 'Kreuzige' at the end of No.36 should be noted.

45(23e).   Recitative, Evangelist, Pilate, 'Pilate saith unto them, Shall I crucify your King? (Spricht Pilatus zu ihnen: Soll ich euren König kreuzigen?)'; continuo

These three and a half bars of recitative and the following four bars of chorus determine Jesus's fate. Pilate asks his question sarcastically, perhaps, singing a higher note (top E) on 'King (König)' than has been heard from him since his second attempt to convince the Jews of Jesus's innocence in No.35.

46(23f).   Chorus, 'We have no king but Caesar (Wir haben keinen König denn den Kaiser)'; tutti (oboe II is an oboe d'amore)

The High Priests proclaim these words in three short declamatory phrases, with 'we' sung three times for emphasis. As stated earlier, the music is that of Nos.3, 5 and 29. All three phrases are statements brief and to the point without the contrapuntal elaborations of No.25, which is structurally different, although it uses the same semiquaver theme.

47(23g).   Recitative, Evangelist, 'Then delivered he him (Da überantwortete er ihn)'; continuo

The answer from the priests in No.46 turns the scales for Pilate, and Jesus is delivered over to be crucified. The 'cross shape' of the notation of the melisma on 'crucified (gekreuziget)' is longer than usual.

48(24).   Aria, Bass and Chorus, 'Haste, ye troubled souls (Eilt, ihr angefocht'nen Seelen)'; strings, bassoon and continuo

Conceived on two levels, a solo voice and orchestra with a three-part chorus interrupting with questions as from another dimension, this aria derives from Brockes, although the basic idea of it is embedded in Lutheran tradition (see the many examples of it in the St Matthew Passion discussed below). 'Haste (Eilt)' is depicted in upward scales and syncopated chords (see below), the former being one of the stock figures employed for ideas of this kind in Bach's time, as can be seen in No.13 of the present work, where haste is implicit though not actually mentioned in the text. Like all the extended arias and choruses other than those constructed from or around chorales, this piece is built on the *ritornello* principle; it all derives from the basic statement of material made at the opening which can be broken down and developed, transposed or all or part repeated. It is a form which offers an infinite variety of possibilities and Bach used it constantly as a basis in movements ranging from gigantic choruses such as the openings of the Mass in B minor and the St Matthew Passion to arias on quite a small scale like No.12 in the St Matthew. Here we have an extended example, full of imaginative touches. For instance, the feeling of 'haste' which is given by the close imitation of first violins and continuo in bars 5–8 and subsequently, and the many examples of displacement of normal accents, the first of which occurs in bars 3–4, giving the effect of three duple-time bars in the upper strings while the triple time remains in the continuo.

49(25a). Recitative, Evangelist, 'Where they crucified him (Allda kreuzigten sie ihn)'; continuo

The Evangelist describes the crucifixion. Pilate continues his provocation of the Jews to the end by writing 'Jesus of Nazareth the King of the Jews (Jesus von Nazareth, der Juden König)' as a superscription on the cross. Bach highlights this magnificently by marking the passage slower and scoring it in a strong but rather remote major key (flat submediant).* The words shine out as though written in gold (see Ex.10), partly because of the tonal shift, and partly because, apart from one brief cadence (bars 4–5), the whole number has been and continues in or around minor keys, and is well sprinkled with poignant chords (diminished sevenths). See also numbers 55 and 64, also St Matthew numbers 52 and 67, for the highlighting in a similar manner of quotations from the Old Testament.

Ex. 10: St John No. 49

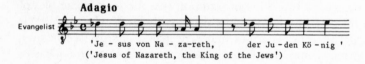

50(25b). Chorus, 'Write not, The King of the Jews (Schreibe nicht: der Juden König)'; tutti

The connection between the text here and that of No.34, whose music is identical, is not so apparent as it was between No.42 and 38. Indeed the verbal stresses are adrift in one or two places—see Ex.11, which shows how the music originally conceived to 'sei grüsset (we greet thee)' just does not fit 'sondern dass er (but that he)'. The general mood is not dissimilar but the semiquaver figures do not have much significance in this context. The common factor 'Juden König' dominates both texts, and the word is embedded in the same notes of the music in both choruses. This completes B^2 of the diagram of the palindrome, No.46 being the first half of it.

*Such terms must be interpreted with flexibility. The passage is rather on a remote chord than in a remote key; and the significance of the word 'key' depends absolutely on its context.

Ex. 11: St John No. 50

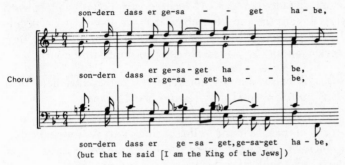

(but that he said [I am the King of the Jews])

51(25c).   Recitative, Evangelist, Pilate, 'Pilate answered, What I have written (Pilatus antwortete: Was ich geschrieben habe)'; continuo

This contains simply Pilate's firm, almost majestic answer to the High Priests' chorus.

52(26).   Chorale, 'In the depths of my heart (In meines Herzens Grunde)'; tutti

The tune is familiar to English church-goers as set to the hymn 'All glory, laud and honour'. Less familiar is Bach's beautiful melisma in phrase 5 on 'picture (Bilde)'* in 'Appear to me in a picture of your bleeding to death, Jesus Christ so mild, as a comfort in my trouble'. The harmonization of the last two phrases beautifully expresses, in this particular context, the thought of innocence suffering to bring comfort to the believer. The chorale verse chosen here is in the first person singular, whereas the previous chorale, No.40, was in the plural. This chorale is A² in the palindrome.

53(27a).   Recitative, Evangelist, 'Then the soldiers (Die Kriegs-knechte aber)'; continuo

Three times in this recitative describing the soldiers' division of Jesus's clothes and explaining why they do not divide his coat

*In English editions, word order is so different from the original German that not infrequently key words such as this are displaced or even omitted.

between them, it could be said that Bach employs realistic phrases. These are: 'Made four parts (Machten vier Teile)'—an upward arpeggio, 'From the top (von oben an)'—a downward arpeggio (as always, compare No.61), and 'And also his coat (dazu auch den Rock)'—a totally jagged phrase (up-down-up-down).

54(27b). Chorus, 'Let us not rend it (Lasset uns den nicht zerteilen)'; tutti (oboe II may be an oboe d'amore)

The soldiers cast lots for Jesus's coat. The realistic portrayal of the rattling of the dice in the 'cello continuo part is unmistakeable; the problem is making it heard through four voice parts, three of which are doubled by strings and wind. This elaborate movement, worked out for fifty-five bars, however fascinating, with all the usual baroque devices of invertible counterpoint and *ritornello* repetitions, seems nevertheless to hold up the recounting of the story, now approaching its climax, for rather too long.

55(27e). Recitative, Evangelist, Jesus, 'That the scripture might be fulfilled (Auf dass erfüllet würde die Schrift)'; continuo

It is interesting here that the quotation from the Old Testament 'They parted my garments among them.... (Sie haben meine Kleide unter sich geteilet...)' is marked *adagio* and set in *quasi-arioso*. In discussing the St Matthew we shall see that Bach similarly changes the style of the *secco* recitative for the Old Testament quotations, although he writes no word into the score to indicate any change in style of performance (see St Matthew Passion, Nos.52 and 67). A theatrically effective, though perhaps not authentic, way of performing these passages is to have them sustained on an organ placed some distance away from the one used for the rest of the recitatives, preferably at the other end of the building. This recitative finishes with Jesus committing his mother and the disciple John to each other; two complementary Words linked by a single phrase from the Evangelist, unified musically because the three phrases are in essence a single harmonic run-up to the final cadence.

56(28). Chorale, 'He took care of all things (Er nahm alles wohl in Acht)'; tutti

The consideration of Jesus for his mother in the Words from the Cross, spoken at the end of No.55, is the subject of the verse here; half-way through the chorale its words apply to mankind in general the lesson that can be drawn from Jesus's consideration. The chord on 'die (stirb)' in the seventh (next to last) phrase is yet another instance of suggesting the meaning of a word through music, even though it sounds ugly in this otherwise beautifully tranquil, because mostly stepwise, chorale. Bach did not go to these lengths in the later Passion.

57(29).   Recitative, Evangelist, Jesus, 'And from that hour (Und von Stund' an)'; continuo

At the very end, Jesus speaks his last Word from the Cross 'It is finished (Es ist vollbracht!)' to a musically dropping phrase which subtly anticipates bowing the head when he passes away in No.59. It also provides the theme for the next movement.

58(30).   Aria, Alto, 'It is finished (Es ist vollbracht)'; free text; viola da gamba, strings, bassoon and continuo

The entirely new tone colour of the viola da gamba, after many movements in which the orchestration has simply alternated between continuo and tutti, makes its due effect here at the crucial moment in the work. The instrument imparts a note of pathos which no other member of the orchestra could do as well. The sudden vivace section, with tutti strings, bassoon and continuo, describing Jesus's victory and finishing the fight '(schliesst den Kampf)' is one of the most dramatic moments in the whole work. The use of a fanfare-like arpeggio in the *vivace* is no accident; it suggests a trumpet call to battle in a characteristically affective manner (cf. No.26 above).

59(31).   Recitative, Evangelist, 'And he bowed his head (Und neigte das Haupt)'; continuo

St John's account of Jesus's death uses the pictorial phrase 'and he bowed his head (und neigte das Haupt)', which is not found in St Matthew's version. Bach's gently falling notes fit the words and the event they describe perfectly. (Cf. Schütz's similarly beautiful treatment of the same words in *The Seven Last Words*.)

60(32).   Aria (Bass), 'My dear Saviour (Mein teurer Heiland)';
free text; and Chorale 'Jesu, who wast killed (Jesu, der du warest
tot)'; strings, continuo and chorus

Bach includes only two two-dimensional movements in this work.
The first (No.48) was in the tradition of interpolating comments,
questions or chorales into a movement, the sense of whose text
doesn't specifically demand them, although it is usually high-
lighted by them (cf. Nos.25, 26, 33, 36 and 70 in the St Matthew).
This movement is rather different. The bass soloist sings an aria
to the dead Jesus and the chorus a chorale in the same spirit, in
no way interrupting the soloist. The effect is certainly two-
dimensional, but the two musical elements run parallel (the
question of whether the chorale singers should come into line
rhythmically with the soloist's groups of three quavers or emphasize their independence by singing duplets is, however, open-
ended). Both elements are tranquil and relaxed. The soloist is
asking questions about what Jesus's death and suffering can do
for him; the chorale singers are not directly answering him, but
rather making their own commentary in a spirit of penitence.
One senses a similar feeling running through this piece to that
which emanates from No.70 in the St Matthew, although in the
latter Jesus is on the Cross but not yet passed away; this
impression could be due to the major key setting common to both
numbers.

61(33).   Recitative, Evangelist, 'And behold (Und siehe da)';
continuo

This account of the rending of the veil of the temple, the
earthquake and saints rising from their graves is not in St John's
Gospel, but, like Peter's weeping in No.18, is here taken straight
from St Matthew's. The music has strong similarities with the
later setting in that certain phrases have to go down—'from the
top to the bottom (von oben an bis unten aus)', and others up;
the declamation of the words is naturally similar, and there is
a rapid downward scale for the rending of the veil and low
repeated semiquavers for the earthquake and its effects, as in the
St Matthew. It paints a telling enough picture, but to anyone
who knows both versions, sounds a little like a trial run for the
later, far more horrific setting.

62(34).   Arioso, Tenor, 'My heart! the whole world suffers with Jesus's suffering (Mein Herz! indem die ganze Welt bei Jesu Leiden gleichfalls leidet)'; free text; two flutes, two oboes da caccia (or oboes d'amore), strings and continuo (no bassoon)

Brockes' words here—as compared to No.32—are free from vulgarity and refer in turn to all the recent events: the darkness, the rending of the veil, the earthquake and rising of the saints from their graves. It was natural that realistic figures would appear in a musical setting of such a text, but Bach allows himself slavishly to follow every descriptive statement by its musical counterpart, and the result is rather pedantic and sometimes even naïve. Nevertheless the atmosphere created by the movement as a whole is fitting enough and the orchestral colour is one not heard before in the work.

63(35).   Aria, Soprano, 'Dissolve O my heart into torrents of tears (Zerfliesse, mein Herze, in Fluten der Zähren)'; free text; flutes, oboes da caccia and continuo

This too gives a new sound, different from any other in either Passion, but No.58 in the St Matthew Passion is related to it; here however all participants share the musical theme, weaving a fascinating four-part linear texture. The words, again derived from Brockes, are expressive, and contain the kind of imagery which composers of the time, including Bach, found inspiring (e.g. 'torrents of tears'; cf. 'heaven-scented flowers' in No.31).

64(36).   Recitative, Evangelist, 'The Jews therefore (Die Juden aber)'; continuo

At the end of this recitative there are two more Old Testament quotations, both of which are given special emphasis, as were those in Nos.49 and 55.

65(37).   Chorale, 'Help, O Christ, Son of God (O hilf, Christe, Gottes Sohn)'; tutti

Bach carries out his purpose of interpreting Bible and hymn words so as to highlight their underlying (or obvious) spiritual message with great force, but perfect control here. There are no forced twists of harmony, yet not a point is missed. The harmonies on 'bitter' (same word in German) and 'vice (Untugend)' are good examples.

66(38).   Recitative, Evangelist, 'And after this Joseph of Arimathaea besought Pilate (Danach bat Pilatum Joseph von Arimathia)'; continuo

The final section of St John's account of the Passion is interesting in that it contains the only reference in all four Gospels to the visit of Nicodemus with spices to the tomb. Melismas are always used for special words or special places, and Bach writes two into the last phrase so as to make a convincing end to the narration.

67(39).   Chorus, 'Rest well, ye holy limbs (Ruht wohl, ihr heiligen Gebeine)'; free text; tutti

The closing *Da Capo* chorus bidding Jesus 'Rest well' is in a well-established tradition. The anonymous (?Böhm) St John Passion of 1704, formerly attributed to Handel, closes with a chorus 'Sleep well (Schlafe wohl)' set to a theme uncannily like that of this movement (see Ex.12). At least, it would be uncanny were it not fairly certain that Bach knew the work, as well as the other Hamburg Passions composed on similar lines. Bach treats the text with great sensitivity; he is able to preserve a mood of tranquillity throughout the movement, as, unlike the case of the chorus closing the St Matthew, there is no 'calling' to Jesus in the grave to suggest anything loud in the character of the music. Even the reference to the Christian's passage to heaven, although soaring upwards, is lightly treated: the first time within the context of the main 'Ruht wohl' music; the second, at higher pitch, with the voices reduced to three and without continuo except for two short phrases.

Ex. 12: Anon. (?Böhm): St John 1704   J.S. Bach: St John No. 67

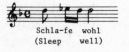

Schla-fe   wohl
(Sleep   well)

Ruht   wohl,   ruht   wohl
(Rest   well,   rest   well)

68(40).   Chorale, 'Ah, Lord, let thy little angel (Ach Herr, lass dein lieb' Engelein)'; tutti

Far from being the anticlimax that a chorale following a long *Da Capo* closing chorus might be, the choice of hymn verse and melody for this movement seems so fitting that the opposite effect is achieved. It presents the idea of human death and resurrection in colourful, emotive words, with music which, although of course traditional as far as melody is concerned, through its pitch and harmonization can make an overwhelmingly dramatic and convincing ending to the whole work. It is remarkable that this third verse of Martin Schalling's sixteenth-century hymn for the dying 'Herzlich Lieb' hab ich dich, O Herr' fits Bernard Schmidt's melody dating from the same period so well. The first section, about rest in the grave, is tranquil with its plagal cadences and soaring phrase for sopranos for the soul being carried to Abraham's bosom. The second section, to words about rising from the grave and the joy of eternal life, is in dramatic contrast: six out of seven of the cadences are perfect and in the major key; this gives the music its incredible strength and majesty; the one imperfect cadence is in minor tonality and is aptly associated with the interpolated prayer 'O Jesu Christ hear me'.

One other setting by Bach of these words to this tune excels this one, namely that which closes the Michaelmas Cantata No.149; here the harmonies are even more chromatic and subtly expressive, and the final phrase is given a sudden lift by a fanfare from three trumpets and timpani, something which would have contravened every rule governing the affections associated with baroque Passion music, had it been introduced here.

6
The Music of the St Matthew Passion

The St Matthew Passion is laid out on a huge scale, judged by any standards, past or present. The forces called for are two four-part choruses, an extra soprano chorus to sing the *ripieno* chorale in the first movement, and two orchestras, each consisting of two flutes, two oboes, bassoon, the usual strings and organ (making two organs altogether). The first orchestra always plays with Choir I and the second with Choir II. Extra instruments include a viola de gamba and two recorders; three different kinds of oboes are also needed. Probably one player 'doubled' on other instruments (for example the recorders were said to have been played by violinists), but even so, the number of players involved is formidable. Bach scored for soprano, alto, tenor and bass soloists from each chorus, plus an Evangelist (tenor) and Jesus (bass) from Choir I. Apart from the last two named, these singers were responsible for the arias and accompanied (and certain *secco*) recitatives and the minor characters. They were the Concertists referred to in Chapter 3, ten of them in all.

The deployment of these forces follows a plan: the first and second choirs, when used separately, represent respectively the twelve disciples and a wider company of believers, except in No.71; both participate in the *turba* or crowd choruses, all of which are scored for a double choir, except in the death scene (No.71) where 'some of them that stood there' are represented by Choir I alone singing 'He calleth for Elias', and 'the rest' by Choir II who respond after a few bars with 'Let be, let us see if Elias will come to save him'. Both groups participate as a double chorus in the introductory movement to Part I (that is No.1), in the closing chorus of Part II and in the second half of No.33. All forces unite in the chorales and in the chorale fantasia which closes Part I, and when doubling each other in these movements represent the whole Christian Church. The Gospel narrations when set as *secco* recitative are with continuo only; the words of Jesus are not *secco* but, following tradition, accompanied by strings (but see below *re* No.71). The terms 'Chorus I' and 'Chorus II' will here refer to the vocal group or individual, or to the instrumental group, or to both.

The St Matthew Passion is more reflective in character than the St John; it contains a very large number of interpolations which interrupt the biblical narrative; there are fourteen chorales (fifteen with the repetition of No.63), eleven accompanied recitatives and fifteen arias. These interpolations are chosen with the utmost skill, and are inserted at very carefully chosen places, not all of which are traditional, and contribute much to the deep spiritual quality which the work possesses. Furthermore, the accompanied recitatives and arias occasionally serve as necessary relief from the tension which builds up as the drama moves inexorably towards its climax.

Part I begins in E minor and finishes in E major; Part II starts in B minor and finishes in C minor. Although the scene of the preparation of the Passover begins and ends in the same key (G major), few others do so. Broadly speaking, Part I is written in sharp keys, except for the first part of the Gethsemane scene. Part II moves gradually through mainly sharp keys until after Jesus's condemnation (end of No.59), when it goes gradually into flatter keys, albeit with one excursion outside them. The death scene itself (No.71 to the middle of 73, if one includes the events that immediately follow the death) starts in E flat and finishes in A flat.

From this analysis, and from what was said in the previous chapter about the tonal schemes of the St John and certain works of Handel, it does not seem to the present writer that any definite general conclusions can be drawn from Bach's use of keys in the Passions. Obviously certain moods are better depicted by some keys than others, but with such long works written without the constrictions that brass instruments would have imposed, Bach seems to have felt remarkably free.

PART I

1.   Double Chorus, 'Come, ye daughters (Kommt, ihr Töchter)'; free text; Orchestra I flutes, oboes, strings and continuo; Orchestra

II flutes, oboes, strings and continuo; (the whole double group = tutti); with Chorale, *ripieno* sopranos, 'O spotless Lamb of God (O Lamm Gottes unschuldig)'; doubled by Organs I and II

This is a gigantic double chorus, over the top of which soars the chorale 'O guiltless Lamb of God' sung by an extra soprano *ripieno* chorus. 'Come, ye daughters, help my crying, see the Bridegroom, see him as a Lamb', cries Choir I. The shouts of 'See', 'See him' provoke the second choir's questions 'Whom?' 'How?' 'What?' Schweitzer sees this chorus as a picture of crowds 'surging through the streets, moving about excitedly, roaring', [1] and the music is so full of movement that any other interpretation seems difficult to imagine. However, viewing the chorus as an expression of grief and treating it quietly and delicately as a Siciliana could also be valid. Structurally the movement is based on a huge *ritornello*, not unlike that of the Kyrie and many other parts of the Mass in B minor. The strength and passion which emanate so powerfully from the music in large measure stem respectively from the nature of the bass line—long pedal points alternating with slow step movement, quick ascending scales—and the nature of the chromatic harmony; it is worth noting that the harmonic basis of the opening theme consists simply of the three principle chords of the key, but so bedecked with every imaginable chromatic embellishment and suspended dissonance that their fundamental simplicity seems scarcely credible. This is the basis of Bach's technique in thousands of works, but it is never more effectively applied than here.

2.   Recitative, Evangelist, Jesus 'When Jesus had finished all these sayings (Da Jesus diese Rede vollendet hatte)'; I strings and continuo

Jesus foretells his crucifixion; the melody set to 'crucified (gekreuziget)', as one would expect, resembles, as far as is musically possible, the shape of a cross.

3.   Chorale, 'O blessed Jesu (Herzliebster Jesu)'; tutti

This answers Jesus's foretelling of his death with the question 'What hast thou done to deserve such punishment?' There is a poignant discord on 'misdeeds (Missetaten)'.

4(4a). Recitative, Evangelist, 'Then assembled together the chief priests (Da versammelten sich die Hohenpriester)'; I continuo

The Evangelist announces the Jews' plan to kill Jesus. There is a sudden twist to C major at the end (the movement begins in D major), perhaps to anticipate the disruptive effect of the following chorus.

5(4b). Double chorus, 'Not on the feast day (Ja nicht auf das Fest)'; tutti

The Jews' fear of a riot by the people if Jesus is seized on a Feast day is immediately evident in this brief double chorus with its swirling figure (bar 3)—see Ex.13—and tremendous upward-driving scale at the end, both expressing 'uproar (Aufruhr)'. The vivid picture created here stems also from the quick interchanges between the two groups at the beginning.

Ex. 13: St Matthew No. 5

6(4c). Recitative, Evangelist, 'Now when Jesus was in Bethany (Da nun Jesus war zu Bethanien)'; I continuo

The Evangelist tells of the woman anointing Jesus with costly ointment; the music of Bach's *secco* recitative expands and enriches traditional melodic formulas as no one else has done before or since. Here, for example, note the expressively descriptive music for 'precious ointment (köstlichem Wasser)'—a chromatic *cantabile* passage, 'and poured it on his head (und goss es auf sein Haupt)'—a downward arpeggio; this is followed by ugly chromatic intervals (tritone and diminished third) at high pitch to express the indignation which the woman's act of devotion is said by the Evangelist to have provoked from the disciples.

7(4d).   Chorus (I), 'To what purpose is this waste (Wozu dienet dieser Unrat)'; I flutes, oboes, strings and continuo

This indignation is expressed in short jagged phrases, followed by a five-part *fugato*—the fifth voice is flutes—with subtly chromatic harmony and melodic angularity at the end.

8(4e).   Recitative, Evangelist, Jesus 'When Jesus understood it (Da das Jesus merkete)'; I strings and continuo

Jesus rebukes the disciples, calmly and firmly; when he relates the anointing to his burial the music sinks with thick quaver chords for '(she did it) for my burial (begraben wird)'; but as he foretells in the closing phrases that the woman's deed will be immortalized by being told wherever the Gospel is preached, the music becomes more animated and majestic.

9(5).   Recitative, Alto, 'Thou dear Saviour, thou (Du lieber Heiland du)'; free text; I flutes and continuo

The four-note motif played by the flutes (without a break through the whole movement) may depict the flowing tears mentioned in the last phrase. This is the first of the interpolations apart from the chorale, No.3, and like most of the solo numbers is very personal in the emotions which it expresses. Mány religious works at this time, and especially Passions, in their pursuit of personalized emotion under the impact of Pietism, introduced allegorical characters like the Believing Soul and the Daughter of Zion. The latter was extremely popular (see No.36) and one can detect something of the emotions traditionally attributed to this character in the present and the following movement.

10(6).   Aria, Alto, 'Contrition and repentance (Buss und Reu)'; free text; I flutes and continuo

The opening melody is a variation of the four-note motif in No.9. The singer bewails his/her sins to music which is in the form of a Minuet (see mention in Chapter I of the dance element prevalent in so many baroque movements). The middle section is miraculously realistic with its overlapping downward arpeggios, marked *staccato*, for the flutes on 'drops', that is, teardrops

('Tropfen'). Whether or not Bach thought of this as a Daughter of Zion aria, and whatever decision we may take today as to whether a counter-tenor or a contralto should sing it, we should remember that it was originally conceived for a young male singer.

11(7).   Recitative, Evangelist, Judas (bass), 'Then one of the twelve... went (Da ging hin der Zwölfen einer)'; I continuo

Judas Iscariot goes to the High Priests and agrees to betray Jesus for thirty pieces of silver. Musically, the wonderfully lyrical final phrase seems rather at odds with the words 'he sought opportunity to betray him'. The subject of this movement is the inspiration for the following number.

12(8).   Aria, Soprano, 'Only bleed, dear heart (Blute nur, du liebes Herz)'; free text; II flutes, strings and continuo

Here the singer declares that a loving heart can only bleed at the thought of Jesus's betrayal. The falling motif of the flutes and strings in the first section is a characteristically baroque expression of grief. In the second half verbal and musical reference is made to Judas as a serpent (note the curling of the *basso-continuo* line in the last five bars).

13(9a).   Recitative, Evangelist, 'Now the first day of the feast of unleavened bread (Aber am ersten Tage der süssen Brot); I continuo; and
14(9b).   Chorus I 'Where wilt thou that we prepare for thee (Wo willst du, dass wir dir bereiten)'; I oboe, strings and continuo

In No.14 the disciples eagerly ask where they shall eat the Passover. Jesus answers in the following number. The music is happy with its fresh, buoyant rhythms. (The disciples have not yet understood Jesus's foretelling of his imminent suffering.) This little chorus falls naturally into two phrases, the first six bars long but the second only five bars, stopping on the dominant chord, the feeling being that the phrase and cadence are completed in the first bar of No.15, just as the words of No.15 also answer the question asked in No.14.

15(9c).   Recitative, Evangelist, Jesus, 'And he said, Go into the city (Er sprach; Gehet hin in die Stadt)'; Chorus I, 'Lord, is it I? (Herr, bin ich's?)'; I strings and continuo

At the crucial moment at the Last Supper, the word 'betray (verraten)' has suitably strange harmony and a short melisma. A profoundly gloomy chord follows (B flat minor after C minor), portraying the disciples' grief, and in the brief closing chorus the question is asked with increasing anxiety 'Lord, is it I? (Herr, bin ich's?). It is significant that the whole phrase 'Herr, bin ich's?' is sung eleven times: there are twelve disciples and Judas is present, but keeps silent. Number symbolism certainly played a part in Bach's thinking (see Chapter 8), and other examples of it may be noticed in the Passions.

16(10).   Chorale, 'It is I, I should atone (Ich bin's, ich sollte büssen)'; I and II oboes, strings and continuo

In typical Lutheran fashion the whole chorus, representing Christians everywhere, immediately becomes personally involved: 'I am (guilty), I should atone (büssen)'. This treatment of the situation can have an overwhelmingly dramatic effect, for Bach has pitched the chorale fairly high, which enables him to use the most effective register of the lower voices, and there is a strident discord on 'büssen' in the third bar.

17(11).   Recitative, Evangelist, Jesus, Judas, 'And he answered and said (Er antwortete and sprach)'; I strings and continuo

Jesus's answer to the question 'Lord, is it I? asked at the end of No.15 is quite relaxed at first, but one might imagine a touch of scarcely suppressed anger in the high *tessitura* of 'it had been good for that man if he had not been born (Es wäre ihm besser, dass derselbige Mensch noch nie geboren wäre)'. This provokes Judas to ask 'Master, is it I?' Jesus's answer is terse: 'Thou hast said.' But Bach makes it slow and thoughtful by clothing the passage with four pairs of flowing quavers in the strings. The institution of the Eucharist follows: Jesus sings a long buoyant arioso in lilting 6-4 time: 'This is my blood of the New Testament (Das ist mein Blut...)', finishing triumphantly: 'in my Father's kingdom (in meines Vaters Reich)'. The fluent *basso-continuo* line of the last five bars with its majestically descending scale contributes to the painting of this scene.

18(12).   Recitative, Soprano, 'Although my heart swims in tears (Wiewohl mein Herz in Tränen schwimmt)'; free text; I oboes d'amore and continuo

In this interpolation the singer's words focus on the joyful aspects of Jesus's sacrifice and on his unending love, but the six-note motif played throughout on the two oboes is announced with the singer's 'although my heart swims in tears', so it has unhappy associations. Indeed, from its shape (see Ex.14) it could derive from the kind of movement suggested by the word 'swims (schwimmt)'. In the hands of other composers such touches—if this is indeed the meaning—can sound naïve, but this piece is so beautifully wrought that the general meaning is clear, whatever individual interpretation may be put on any particular motif.

Ex. 14: St Matthew No. 18

19(13).   Aria, Soprano, 'I will give thee my heart (Ich will dir mein Herze schenken)'; free text; I two oboes d'amore and continuo

In this happy aria the oboes announce an embellished version of the soprano's opening melody. The continuo line is almost entirely independent of the tunes given to oboes and voice. The nature of this movement and its placing give brief but welcome relief from the predominantly sombre mood.

20(14).   Recitative, Evangelist, Jesus, 'And when they had sung an hymn (Und da sie den Lobgesang gesprochen hatten)'; I strings and continuo

This recitative is set in the garden of Gethsemane; in it Jesus warns his disciples that they will 'be offended because of me (ärgern an mir) this night'. It contains two tone pictures. The first is the seven-note upward scale in the continuo at the end of bar 2; it must have a specific meaning or it is ridiculous; as the voice continues the scale upwards for another six steps in bar 3 to the words 'they went out' (or 'up') 'into the Mount of Olives', the immediate impression is that the whole thirteen-note scale describes the ascent of the mount. Alternatively, it might conceivably refer to the hymn singing mentioned in the first sentence. The important point is that such a figure occurring in a *secco* recitative *is* unusual and must have an association and be given due attention in performance. This applies far more to the passage of rapid staccato semiquaver chords for all the strings six bars later at 'and the sheep... shall be scattered': this exaggerated but enormously effective picture breaks in so suddenly that the most inattentive listener's concentration is immediately recalled to what is going on.

21(15).   Chorale, 'Look upon me, my guardian (Erkenne mich, mein Hüter)'; tutti

This is the first appearance of the 'Passion Chorale', so called because of its frequent occurrences in this work. It is harmonized simply, but its more expressive moments are really more suited to the words of No.23 (q.v.; and see also Appendix for the origin of this chorale and the words of Nos 21 and 23).

22(16).   Recitative, Evangelist, Jesus, Peter (Bass), 'Peter answered (Petrus aber antwortete)'; I strings and continuo

Here occur Peter's two protests (responding to Jesus's warning in No.20) that he will never deny his Master; the second is higher and more agitated than the first and punctuated with quick-moving continuo chords.

23(17).   Chorale, 'I will stand here beside thee (Ich will hier bei dir stehen)'; I and II oboes, strings and continuo

The whole chorus, although usually somewhat detached from the drama in the chorales, becomes very involved here, responding to the words of Peter and 'all the disciples' that they will never deny Jesus with 'I will stand here beside thee. . .' The harmony of the Passion Chorale here is identical with that of No.21, and it contains beautiful word-painting on 'the last death-agony (letzten Todesstoss)' with a sharp dissonance on 'Tod-' in the sixth phrase.

24(18).   Recitative, Evangelist, Jesus, 'Then cometh Jesus with them (Da kam Jesus mit ihnen)'; I strings and continuo

Jesus's agony in Gethsemane calls forth profoundly sorrowful music, expressed through a twisting chromatic phrase on 'and began to be sorrowful (und fing an zu trauern)', but there are other striking features too. A bar of beautiful arioso is given to 'pray (bete)', and the throbbing strings at the end vividly express the emotion of 'My soul is exceeding sorrowful, even unto death'—note the low note on 'death (Tod)'. Bach's setting of this phrase using the traditional throbbing quavers is paralleled for example in R. Keiser's St Mark Passion (which Bach performed and partly copied out); Keiser's setting is far less moving in its impact than Bach's, however; it includes one rather empty sequence, and his use of the well-worn descending chromatic bass does not produce anything unexpected. The first three and a half bars of Bach's movement are based entirely on one chord (F), perhaps to give the impression of the darkness that must have enshrouded Gethsemane when Jesus and the disciples reached it.

25(19).   Recitative, Tenor, 'O pain, here trembles the tortured heart! (O Schmerz! hier zittert das gequälte Herz!); free text; with Chorale, Chorus II, 'What is the cause of all such torment? (Was ist die Ursach' aller solcher Plagen?)'; I recorders, oboes da caccia and continuo, II strings and continuo

Here we have the first of several examples in this work of music laid out on two levels. The first tenor soloist, with a plaintive combination of instruments from Orchestra I, intertwining with a dissonant figure over a throbbing pedal, sings of Jesus's bitter grief, trembling and bringing to judgment; he asks whether the overwhelming love which he bears his Saviour cannot bring relief by helping to carry the burden. All this is broken up by the voices of Choir II singing, as from another dimension, an embellished version of the chorale tune heard in No.3: 'What is the cause of all such torment?' The continuously throbbing bass pedal in semiquavers was the traditional baroque way of expressing feelings like anxiety, and the tenor soloist's *tessitura* is very high; in contrast, the music of Choir II is very low and subdued. The manner in which the last phrase of the chorale avoids finality by sliding into the throbbing bass of the recitative is very effective. The strikingly diverse sounds of the recitative and chorale make this movement a high emotional point in the unfolding of the drama.

26(20).   Aria, Tenor, 'I will watch with Jesus (Ich will bei meinem Jesu wachen)'; with Chorus II, 'And so our sins will fall asleep (So schlafen unsre Sünden ein)'; free texts; I oboe and continuo, II flutes, strings and continuo

The two-dimensional structure and the same vocal forces continue here, but there are changes in orchestration. The keyword is 'watch' and the solo oboe announces a theme based on a traditional watchman's call (see Ex.15); it is interesting that in bar 3 the oboe borrows a four-note idea from the as yet unheard music of Choir II associated with 'and so our sins will fall asleep'. But the contrast between the quasi-lullaby character of most of Choir II's music and the forthright yet emotionally charged melodies of Choir I is the most important aspect of the movement.

Ex. 15: St Matthew No. 26

27(21).   Recitative, Evangelist, Jesus, 'And he went a little farther (Und ging hin ein wenig)'; I strings and continuo

Jesus falls down on his face in prayer (the vocal line naturally drops too): 'O my Father, if it be possible, let this cup pass from me...'

28(22).   Recitative, Bass, 'The Saviour falls down before his Father (Der Heiland fällt vor seinem Vater nieder)'; free text; II strings and continuo

This comments with a falling figure in all the upper strings, played incessantly and at regular intervals except once, at the words 'up to God's grace', when it changes direction.

29(23).   Aria, Bass, 'Willingly will I submit (Gerne will ich mich bequemen)'; free text; II strings and continuo

This aria contains splendid sweeping phrases played on all the violins and, with the previous number, creates quite a long, undramatic break in the scene in the Garden of Gethsemane. But the change of thought which it provides is nicely calculated; we need such a break before the scene rushes to its climax in Nos 32 and 33.

30(24). Recitative, Evangelist, Jesus, 'And he cometh unto the disciples (Und er kam zu seinen Jüngern)'; I strings and continuo

The words and music of Jesus's first prayer (No.27) are transposed upwards and embellished, and thereby intensified here when, in deeper anguish, he repeats it.

31(25).   Chorale, 'What my God wills (Was mein Gott will)'; tutti

This chorale is particularly appropriate here, as its text contains almost the same words as those used by Jesus at the end of No.30, 'Thy will be done (so geschehe dein Wille)'. The particularly strong cadence (dominant and tonic progressions) attached to the last two phrases underlines the strong conviction of the words.

32(26).   Recitative, Evangelist, Jesus, Judas, 'And he came and found them asleep again (Und er kam und fand sie aber schlafend)'; I strings and continuo

In spite of his warning ('Watch and pray') in No.30, Jesus finds the disciples asleep again—the musical phrase is almost identical with that of No.30 (see Ex.16). When he returns to the disciples after going away to pray a third time, the action and music quicken. A 'great multitude (eine grosse Schar)' arrives from the chief priests and elders, led by Judas Iscariot. Jesus is seized and led into Jerusalem, but not before he has challenged Judas to say why he has come—a sustained chord and a relaxed phrase beginning 'Friend... (Mein Freund...)'.

Ex. 16a: St Matthew No. 30

Und er kam zu sein-en Jüng-ern, und fand sie schla-fend
(And he came to his disciples and found them sleeping)

Ex. 16b: St Matthew No. 32

Und er kam und fand sie a – ber schla-fend
(And he came and found them asleep again)

33(27a and b).   Duet, Soprano, Alto, 'My Jesus now is taken (So ist mein Jesus nun gefangen)'; with Chorus II, 'Leave him, stop! (Lasst ihn, haltet!)'; leading to Double Chorus, 'Have lightnings and thunders vanished into the clouds? (Sind Blitze, sind Donner in Wolken verschwunden?)'; free texts

In the East, women were traditionally hired to lament when an occasion called for it. This duet for soprano and alto soloists without continuo could be a realistic and greatly transcended version of such wailing, or it could represent two of the disciples. The woodwind ornaments give the piece its character, and if the singers do not copy them just because they happen to be written into the instrumental and not into the vocal parts, the effect is weakened. The Lamentation is three times assailed by Chorus

II with shouts of 'Loose him, stop, (Lasst ihn, haltet, bindet nicht!)'. This is the most dramatic treatment imaginable of a Lutheran tradition, examples of which were first heard in milder form in Nos 25 and 26. The second, double chorus section, 'Have lightnings and thunders vanished into the clouds? (Sind Blitze, sind Donner in Wolken verschwunden?)' is, to quote Geiringer, 'One of the most violent and grandiose descriptions of unloosed passion produced in the baroque era'.[2] The sharp contrast with the duet and its lack of a basso continuo, incessant semiquavers in the continuo, shrieking woodwind, scales and arpeggios, and choral writing which includes *fugato* (imitation) and strong chordal hammerstrokes all contribute to the unique effect produced by this extraordinary movement.

34(28).   Recitative, Evangelist, Jesus, 'And behold, one of them (Und siehe, Einer aus denen)'; I strings and continuo

The setting of the final moments before Jesus reaches the palace of the High Priest contains as many varied ideas as does the text itself. The description of cutting off the servant's ear in bars 4 and 5—a zigzag phrase moving up a fourth, down a third, up a second and down a fourth—and Jesus's reminder at the end that his arrest was foretold by the prophets—three smooth shapely phrases based on slow-moving diatonic harmony—are particularly fine examples of baroque expression.

35(29).   Chorale, 'O man, bewail thy great sin (O Mensch, bewein' dein' Sünde gross)'; tutti

This is an extended chorale fantasia whose text exhorts mankind to bewail its sins and repent and tells of the manifold sufferings of Jesus, and of the good he did. The orchestral music, which is quite independent of the voices, is based on comparatively few musical figures. The principal motif is announced by the flutes and carried mainly by them throughout the movement; it is a passage of semiquavers grouped in twos in step movement, traditionally associated, particularly in its downward moving form, with sighing. The music of this fantasia is so poignant and emotive that far from there being any impression of monotony, one feels that such a movement could go on endlessly.

PART II

36(30). Aria, Alto, 'Ah, now my Jesus is gone (Ach, nun ist mein Jesus hin)'; with Chorus II, 'Where is thy friend gone? (Wo ist denn dein Freund hingegangen?)'; free texts; I flute, oboe d'amore, strings and continuo, II strings and continuo

Part II begins with another two-dimensional movement, but here the quasi-mystical separation of the groups which was the characteristic feature of Nos 25 and 26 is not so apparent; indeed the soloist from the first chorus and the chorus from the second are interlocked in something like a conversation. The soloist, whose personality is closely akin to that of the traditional Daughter of Zion (see Nos 9 and 10), is distraught; the choir tries to comfort her. Of all the interpolated movements in the St Matthew, this is the most personal. Agitation is felt in the rapid upward scales, suspended discords, and often chromatically falling intervals (appoggiaturas) in a minor tonality allotted to the soloist; in contrast, comfort seems to emanate from the chorus because their music in general lacks dissonance and two out of three sections are in the major key.

37(31). Recitative, Evangelist, 'And they that had laid hold on Jesus (Die aber Jesum gegriffen hatten)'; I continuo

Continuing the narration, the Evangelist brings us to the point where the Jews sought false witnesses against Jesus. The music of the penultimate phrase, 'auf dass sie ihn tödteten (to put him to death)', is suddenly angular, exploring all the notes of a diminished seventh. A personal protest is provoked in the next number.

38(32). Chorale, 'The world has betrayed me (Mir hat die Welt trüglich gericht't)'; tutti

Combined forces, accusing the world of similarly treacherous accusations, pray for protection against such evils. The chromatic harmony on 'lies (Lügen)' and the change to a more relaxed style for the last five bars, namely the prayer, are striking.

39(33). Recitative, Evangelist, False Witnesses (Alto and Tenor), High Priest (Bass), 'Though many false witnesses came (Und wiewohl viel falsche Zeugen herzutraten)'; I continuo, II continuo

Much has been made of the realistic and effective idea of making the two false witnesses sing the same tune and words one behind the other; however, this had been done before, for example, by Heinrich Schütz in his St Matthew Passion of 1666. Many other illuminating devices in both Bach's Passions have similar traditional origins: two that immediately spring to mind are the melisma associated with the cock crowing, and the continuo's repeated semiquavers for the earthquake. But Bach made these traditional devices come alive to an extent that none of his predecessors was able to do; here for example, the ironical ascending passage on 'build (bauen)' when the false witnesses accuse Jesus of having said that he could destroy the Temple and rebuild it in three days is remarkable in that it doesn't just go up the scale, but consists of a series of zigzag steps—two up and one down, quite rough in effect.

40(34). Recitative, Tenor, 'My Jesus keeps silence (Mein Jesus schweigt)'; free text; II oboes and continuo

Jesus's dignified silence is strongly reflected in the music, the orchestral portion of which is nothing but a series of chords, each separated by a half beat's silence, an instance of a realistic device that seems inextricably wedded to this particular text (see the discussion of this point in Chapter 3; and cf. the bass recitative in Cantata No.61 for another example). For a later performance when the organ which should have accompanied Choir II was not available, Bach reinforced the substituting harpsichord continuo with a *pizzicato* gamba. To use it when conditions are normal tends to encroach on the vital silences between the chords.

41(35). Aria, Tenor, 'Patience, when false tongues sting me (Geduld! wenn mich falsche Zungen stechen)'; free text; II continuo

For the reason mentioned above (see No.40) Bach also scored a gamba to reinforce the 'cello for a later performance. Unlike most other arias in this work, this music contains two highly contrasted ideas within the announcing phrase played by the continuo; their meaning is obvious; smooth, shapely quavers to express 'patience (Geduld)' under the accusations of the 'false tongues (falsche Zungen)', which have violently jagged, dotted semiquavers and demisemiquavers; and auxiliary ideas also have pictorial treatment, for example 'revenge (rächen)' in bars 25–27.

42(36a and 36b).   Recitative, Evangelist, Jesus, High Priest and Double Chorus, 'And the High Priest answered. . . I adjure thee (Und der Hohepriester antwortete. . . Ich beschwöre dich)'; tutti

Jesus's music in this movement, his last extended recitative-arioso in the work, includes a wonderfully buoyant string accompaniment for 'coming in the clouds of Heaven (kommen in den Wolken des Himmels)' and ends with a very concise double chorus 'He is guilty of death (Er ist des Todes schuldig)'. In a few seconds a build-up is made from a single low-pitched note to a high-pitched shriek, climaxing in an eight-part texture. Thus declamation, texture and pitch combine to bring out the force of the words—the last word in the German being 'guilty (schuldig)'. One often regrets that Bach did not compose an opera as such, but in the Passions there is everything operatic barring the stage directions.

43(36c and 36d).   Recitative, Evangelist and Double Chorus, 'Then did they spit in his face (Da speieten sie aus in sein Angesicht)'; tutti

The mocking double chorus 'Prophesy unto us, thou Christ, Who is he that smote thee?' which concludes this short movement (some editions place it at the beginning) is a picture of a different sort: two scurrilous groups vying with each other in interlocking alternation of short phrases as to who can insult the prisoner with the loudest and most venomous notes, yet in effect they are singing the same music.

44(36).   Chorale, 'Who has struck thee thus (Wer hat dich so geschlagen)'; tutti

In exactly the same peculiarly Lutheran manner as that in which the full chorus of believers in No.16 answers the disciples' question 'Lord, is it I?' of No.15, so the same group here immediately repeats the question asked by the crowd in No.43. Bach gives his chorus just one beat's rest in which to change from being Jesus's vindictive enemies in No.43 to representing his adoring followers in this chorale.

45(38a and 38b).   Recitative, Evangelist, First Maid (soprano), Second Maid (alto), Peter and Chorus II, 'Now Peter sat without in the palace (Petrus aber sass draussen im Palast)'; I continuo, II flutes, oboes, strings and continuo

This contains Peter's first two denials, the first quite mild, the second higher and more angular. Schweitzer's suggestion makes sense that in the repeated semiquavers of the orchestra in the chorus 'Surely thou also art one of them' mocking laughter can be heard.[2]

46(38c).   Recitative, Evangelist, Peter, 'Then began he to curse and to swear (Da hub er an sich zu verfluchen und zu schwören)'; continuo

The third denial is not intrinsically more emphatic than the second, though it can be made to sound so and the context strengthens the total effect. This movement is distinguished by some of Bach's most inspired recitative writing, descriptive and expressive, but never to excess (cf. Peter's weeping in the St John Passion).

47(39).   Aria, Alto, 'Have mercy on me, my God (Erbarme dich, mein Gott)'; free text; I solo violin, strings and continuo

The surpassing beauty of this piece lies in the subtly changing harmonies, the incessant *pizzicato* bass and, above all, in the ornamentation, not all of which is written into the score, and has therefore to be worked out by analogy to achieve a satisfactory performance. This in fact applies to most pieces of baroque music, but it is more vital here than in most cases.*

48(40).   Chorale, 'If I have wandered from thee (Bin ich gleich von dir gewichen)'; tutti

Again the chorale responds to what the singer has been feeling in the previous number; but although it is a fine example of the genre, there is always a danger that it can sound like an anticlimax, because of the contrast between its rather plain harmony and the highly embellished melodies and chromaticism of No.47.

49(41a and 41b).   Recitative, Evangelist, Judas and Double Chorus, 'When the morning was come (Des Morgens aber)'; tutti

The utter horror that overwhelms Judas when he realizes what he has done can be felt in the chromatic chord that covers 'evil (übel)' in his single statement (bar 14): 'I have sinned ['done evil'] in that I have betrayed the innocent blood (Ich habe übel getan, dass ich unschuldig Blut verraten habe)'. The reply of the high priests and elders 'What is that to us? (Was gehet uns das an?)' is cold and impatient; Bach expresses their impatience through the building up in pitch, texture and harmonic intensity which he achieves in these four short bars of chorus.

50(41c).   Recitative, Evangelist, and Arioso, Two Priests (Basses), 'And he cast down the pieces of silver (Und er warf die Silberlinge)'; I continuo

Judas throws down the money, goes out and hangs himself; every detail of this statement is pictorially reflected, for example in the

---

*The first six notes of the violin obbligato in this piece, including the ornamental slide, are identical with the violin obbligato theme in the first duet of Cantata No.140, but the continuations are different. The text of the Cantata is about blissful mystical love—which serves to show the folly of pursuing thematic relationships too far. When the 'theme' in question consists of standard figures made up from adjacent notes (e.g. just scales) or simple dominant to tonic movement to establish a key, the practice becomes particularly absurd and irrelevant. Such resemblances should not be confused with obvious connections that do make sense, such as that between Nos.9 and 10 discussed above.

Ex. 17: St Matthew No. 50

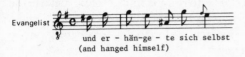

und er - hän-ge - te sich selbst
(and hanged himself)

jagged shape of the melody Bach has given to selected words (See Ex.17).

51(42).   Aria, Bass, 'Give me back my Jesus (Gebt mir meinen Jesum wieder)'; free text; II solo violin, strings and continuo

This is the last of the interpolations interrupting the narrative whose music is of a cheerful character. A great deal has been written about the possible meaning of the solo violin's theme, with its rushing upward scales and the wide span of its arpeggios. If explanation is necessary, the most obvious one is that these features have to do with the rolling away on the Temple floor of the money which Judas has just thrown down. The sentiments of the text and music are certainly fitting to this interpretation.

52(43).   Recitative, Evangelist, Jesus, Pilate, 'And they took counsel (Sie hielten aber einen Rat)'; I strings and continuo

Jesus here utters his last two Words before those delivered from the Cross: they are accompanied by three detached chords, which help to emphasize the significance of his almost total silence during the trial. At the beginning of this number we hear how the Jews spent the money that Judas returned (see No.50 which explains that because it was tainted they could not put it into the Treasury). The following passage (bars 10 to 16), referring to the fulfilment of Jeremiah's prophecy, is one of the most beautiful passages of recitative in the whole work, in fact it is really in quasi-arioso style; the purpose of this change of style being to highlight the fact that this is an interpolation from the Old Testament into the Gospel narrative (see also No.67).

53(44).   Chorale, 'Commend thy ways (Befiehl du deine Wege)'; tutti

This chorale, another setting of the 'Passion Chorale', urges the Christian: 'Commend thy ways and what oppresses thy heart to

the all-faithful care of Him who is Heaven's guide.' It is signif-
icantly placed in the scene with Pilate immediately before the
number in which the first cries of 'Let him be crucified' occur.
The scoring is less sonorous here than in earlier versions, partly
because of its lower pitch.

54(45a).   Recitative, Evangelist, Pilate, Pilate's Wife (Soprano)
and Double Chorus, 'Now at that feast (Auf das Fest aber)';
tutti

Pilate's wife makes her only appearance (bars 18–21); in two
phrases—sometimes sung as though they were three!—Bach gives
a graphic impression of her fear about her husband's involvement
in Jesus's trial and probable condemnation, through the high
pitch of her first phrase (giving the impression of strain) and the
chromatic notes relating to her dream. In the middle of the
movement comes the famous shout by both choirs of 'Barabbas':
famous because of its staggeringly effective brevity—indeed, it
could not be briefer. Here Bach, who was not always concise in
his treatment of dramatic moments (cf. several in the St John
Passion), surpasses himself in his feeling for dramatic effect. One
wonders what the conservative Leipzig congregation must have
thought; this shout would certainly have jolted them out of the
sleep of boredom that they were probably enjoying. The late
Bach scholar Walter Emery, also a devoted Wagnerian, once said
to the present writer that this was the one place where Bach
surpassed Wagner. At the close of this movement, the words 'Let
him be crucified' are also treated briefly, though in a different
way. Just one entry of the angularly descriptive theme, the
notation suggesting the shape of a cross, is stated by each voice,
then a climax immediately develops, which is followed by three
silent beats, and then the following chorale.

55(46).   Chorale, 'How amazing is this punishment! (Wie wun-
derbarlich ist doch diese Strafe!)'; tutti

This is a more chromatic and emotional setting of the melody
used in the first four-part chorale in the work, No.3. To express
dazed amazement, before arriving at the end of the phrase the
harmonies screw round in a circle, or to be more precise, two

half-circles, through the basic harmonies of no less than ten chords with grinding chromatic steps in the bass.

56(47).   Recitative, Evangelist, Pilate, 'And the governor said (Der Landpfleger sagte)'; I continuo

Just two bars for Pilate to ask the crucial question 'Why, what evil hath he done?' The answer comes immediately, but not from those of whom it was asked.

57(48).   Recitative, Soprano, 'He has done good to us all (Er hat uns allen wohl getan)'; free text; I oboes da caccia and continuo

The soprano replies in this interpolation; the Jews' answer comes later. She enumerates Jesus's good deeds. Although the obbligato and continuo parts pursue their respective ideas consistently until the penultimate bar, the vocal line paints every emotive word either with melody, harmony or both. Note, for example, the treatment of 'the blind (den Blinden)', with its pathetic diminished seventh, the upward moving phrase on 'he drove out devils (er trieb die Teufel fort)', and in 'the distressed hath he raised up (Betrübte hat er aufgericht't)' the diminished seventh on 'distressed' followed by a more quickly moving upward phrase which reaches the highest note of the piece.

58(49).   Aria, Soprano, 'For love my Saviour will die (Aus Liebe will mein Heiland sterben)'; free text; I flute, oboes da caccia

The texture, orchestral colour and atmosphere created by the music and its scoring produce a piece which is unique not only in this work but probably among all Bach's compositions. It is not only that the continuo is omitted, which is not uncommon in pieces which are intended to suggest a feeling of insecurity, but the intertwining of flute and soprano, with relentlessly repeated crotchet pulses from the oboes (only occasionally relieved by a bar of wailing dotted quavers and semiquavers), and the recurring pauses on various poignant chords, express far better than words could the reaction of a devoted follower to the agony of the Passion.

59(50a, b, c and d). Recitative, Evangelist and Double Chorus, 'But they cried out the more (Sie schrieen aber noch mehr)'; tutti

This recitative, with its surprising opening chord (chromatic in the key of No.58), cuts in immediately, cruelly, on the sorrowful thoughts engendered by the previous number with 'But they cried out the more, saying, Let him be crucified'. Bach simply repeats the music of the first 'Crucify' chorus but highlights the meaning of 'more (noch mehr)' by putting this one up a whole tone, embracing high As for sopranos and tenors, so that it finishes with something like a yell. This number includes two choruses; the second, 'His blood be on us (Sein Blut komme über uns)', is fugal in structure; that is to say one main theme, announced in the bass, but 'covered' by other parts, is tossed from voice to voice, although as most parts are active all the time they are not always easy to hear. In order, the theme comes in the bass, tenor, soprano, alto, bass and soprano. Just before the close of this extended movement (more sensibly numbered in the Neue Bach Ausgabe) the Evangelist refers to the scourging of Jesus. This explains the otherwise inexplicable music of the next number.

60(51). Recitative, Alto, 'Merciful God (Erbarmes Gott)'; free text; II strings and continuo

An incessant, relentless dotted figure in the upper strings gives a realistic impression of scourging, while long notes in the bass, most of them chromatic, give the harmony a suitably dark colour. In bar 11 the singer cries 'Have mercy! Stop!', that is, stop the 'blows' and 'wounds' mentioned in bars 3 and 4, as though they could no longer be suffered; immediately the music cadences on the nearest home chord and stops.

61(52). Aria, Alto, 'Can the tears of my cheeks (Können Tränen meiner Wangen)'; free text; II strings and continuo

More perhaps than any other aria, this one needs expert singing and playing. It is extremely long, but can create a powerful impression of weeping (main vocal theme) at the thought of the scourging (main instrumental theme, echoing the rhythm of No.60)—if the almost insuperable difficulty of maintaining a tight grip on the basic rhythmic pattern throughout 155 bars is overcome. In the middle section, shortly before the *Da Capo*, Bach slides into remote flat keys with moving effect, pausing on one of the most beautifully placed chords of the seventh that even he ever wrote (bar 85), before working back sequentially to a cadence in a more normal key.

62(53a, b and c).   Recitative, Evangelist, and Double Chorus, 'Then the soldiers of the governor took Jesus (Da nahmen die Kriegsknechte des Landpflegers Jesum)'; tutti

Now the crown of thorns is put on Jesus's head and 'they bowed the knee before him (und beugeten die Knie vor ihm)'; note the downward-upward-downward curves of the Evangelist's melody. The crowd in antiphonal manner mocks him in short answering phrases. There is a snarling diminished seventh on the first syllable of '-könig' at the cadence 'King of the Jews (Judenkönig)'.

63(54).   Chorale, 'O head full of blood and wounds (O Haupt voll Blut und Wunden)'; tutti

This is another version of the 'Passion Chorale' (cf. Nos.21, 23, 53), this time to words more specifically focused on the crucifixion itself (cf. the hymn 'O sacred head' in English hymnbooks). Bach has chosen a high pitch here, partly to fit the tonal scheme, but obviously for expressive purposes too.

64(55).   Recitative, Evangelist, 'And after that they had mocked him (Und da sie ihn verspottet hatten)'; I continuo

This short recitative is distinguished by the tender expressiveness of the melisma on 'crucified (kreuzigten)' in bar 5. See Ex.18.

Ex. 18: St Matthew No. 64

65(56).   Recitative, Bass, 'Yes certainly, flesh and blood in us (Ja! freilich will in uns das Fleisch und Blut); free text; I flutes, gamba and continuo

The scoring for two flutes with gamba (its first appearance) and continuo produces another unique sound (cf. No.58) not used anywhere else in Bach's works. Schweitzer seems right here when he says that in the upward and, at the end, downward movement of the flutes we see Jesus 'stumbling forward and at last falling'.[3] See Ex.19.

Ex. 19: St Matthew No. 65

66(57).   Aria, Bass, 'Come, sweet cross (Komm, süsses Kreuz); free text, I gamba and continuo

Underneath the embellishments of the solo gamba's melody is the steady tread of the procession to Calvary. Simon of Cyrene carries the cross (see No.64) and the singer, personifying Christians generally, sings 'Come, sweet cross... Jesus give it me always', which explains perhaps why the music feels basically contented, if not actually happy, despite being in a minor key and interpolated at this dark point in the story.

67(58a, b, c and d).   Recitative, Evangelist and Double Chorus, 'And when they were come unto a place called Golgotha (Und da sie an die Stätte kamen mit Namen Golgatha)'; tutti

The Evangelist tells of the crucifixion. When reference is made to the Old Testament prophecy of the rending of garments and the casting of lots, as before Bach writes in a quasi-arioso style, so that the passage sounds different from the rest of the narration (cf. No.52). The jeering double choruses 'Thou that destroyest the temple' and 'He saved others; himself he cannot save' are venomous in character. Apart from the upward phrase to high B (the highest vocal note in the whole work) on 'and buildest it in three days', most of the musical material consists of stomping downward scales in a short-long-short-long-short-long rhythm to illustrate 'now come down from the cross (so steig herab vom Kreuz)'. But in the closing bars the movement drives on to a tremendous climax: the derisive 'Let him deliver him' cadences in D minor, remote from the basic key of E minor, yet only three bars from the end! But at this point the piece is swung powerfully back home with a sudden and extended dominant chord, and closes with the only unison passage in the whole work, held in reserve until now, so as effectively to emphasize the pompous boastfulness of the mocking 'I am the Son of God (Ich bin Gottes Sohn)'. Bach (or perhaps one of his assistants?) has indicated harmonies for the organ at this point; it seems to be a place—perhaps the only one—where one should ignore the composer's directions in the interests of clear texture, balance and dramatic effect and let the organ also play in unison.

68(58e).   Recitative, Evangelist, 'The thieves also... cast the same in his teeth (Desgleichen schmäheten ihn auch die Mörder)'; I continuo

Even in this brief three-bar recitative Bach not only gives the notation on the words 'crucified with him (mit ihm gekreuziget)' the descriptive up-down-up-down shape but endows the word 'crucified' with a chromatic chord (the 'Neapolitan sixth') reserved for special moments such as the cadences in No.33 and the final farewell in No.77 (soprano voice). Nos.2, 54 and 59 also contain cross-like melodic shapes on this word, so central to the Passion, and it must be borne in mind that this sort of word-painting was an integral part of the baroque method of communication. Today it is easy to underrate its importance and even smile at it, but in so doing one may fail to receive the full impact of the music.

69(59).   Recitative, Alto, 'Ah Golgotha (Ach Golgatha)'; free text; I two oboes da caccia and continuo

The scoring, melody and harmony are dark; everything is placed low. The orchestral scoring is similar to that of No.57, though here the 'cellos are *pizzicato*, but the mood is entirely different; the harmony is lower-pitched, more extravagantly chromatic, the flattened fifth of the B flat seventh and in bar 13 is striking—and a thick gloom prevails. Jesus's death is imminent, and the soloist (?Daughter of Zion) finishes with a very chromatic phrase closing on a dissonance which the instruments resolve. This is uncommon, but not unique; the same sort of thing happens at the end of the chorus in Cantata No.73 to the words 'Lord, as thou wilt', where a whole choir is involved.

70(60).   Aria, Alto, 'Behold, Jesus has stretched out his hands (Sehet, Jesus hat die Hand... ausgespannt)'; with Chorus II; free text; I two oboes da caccia and continuo, II two oboes, strings and continuo

By contrast this number is free from daring chromaticisms and sounds resigned, even contented. Some commentators regard Jesus's love radiating from the Cross as the dominant feeling; probably this is true but the feature which is structurally most important is the return to the two-dimensional scheme used earlier (cf. Nos.25, 26, 33 and 36), a scheme in the tradition that produced No.48 in the St John Passion ('Haste'), which itself was taken from Brockes (see Chapter 1). The alto sings of the salvation emanating from Jesus's arms outstretched on the Cross, and adds 'Come'. This inevitably evokes the literal response 'Where?' from the committed followers, Chorus II; such an exchange was a trait in Lutheran music from the time of the seventeenth-century Hammerschmidt's Dialogues. Musically this is one of the most attractive movements in the whole work. Much of the continuo music and, in a different way, that of the oboes too, is in a rocking-lullaby style, and would seem to be inspired by the words 'stay in Jesu's arms (bleibet in Jesu Armen)'; whenever they occur this style is much in evidence.

71(61a, b, c, d and e).   Recitative, Evangelist, Jesus, Choruses I and II, 'Now from the sixth hour (Und von der sechsten Stunde an)'; I oboes, strings and continuo

The death scene, whose sections must be treated as one, never fails to stagger one through its intensely dramatic but incredibly terse musical treatment. The whole series of events from Jesus's cry 'Eli, Eli, lama sabachthani?', where his string accompaniment deserts him, to his death, is over in the space of one minute. The sequence from No.71 to the end of the chorus of No.73, indeed, is like nothing else one can think of in music in the swiftness and power of its impact. The fact that the melody of 'Eli, Eli . . .' and its translation, and the outburst of Chorus I 'He calleth for Elias', is in each case a common chord may have some significance.

72(62).   Chorale, 'When my time of departing comes (Wenn ich einmal soll scheiden)'; tutti

After Jesus's death, the Passion Chorale follows whose words are a prayer for succour at the hour of death; it is the chorale which was traditionally placed here (cf. Keiser's St Mark Passion, where he sets it as a solo—more personal therefore—with an elaborate continuo accompaniment). Bach's subdued, low-pitched setting makes its effect through its chromatic harmony.

73(63a, b and c).   Recitative, Evangelist and Double Chorus. 'And behold, the veil of the temple (Und siehe da, der Vorhang im Tempel)'; tutti (without flutes)

Immediately, the vividly painted pictures of the rending of the temple veil, the earthquake and the dead saints rising out of their graves crash in one after the other. When one thinks seriously about the nature of these events, no amount of extravagance in describing them would seem unjustifiable, yet Bach does it all with continuo instruments only (scales rushing up and down for the rending of the veil, and horrendous, low, chromatic demi-semiquavers, almost *tremolo*, for the earthquake and rising of the saints); and all this in the space of nine bars, occupying a time-space of thirty seconds! At the terror of the centurion 'and they that were with him' Bach gives the recitative a sudden twist from G minor to A flat major and writes high notes on the words

'feared greatly (erschraken sie sehr)'. In the setting of the words
which they speak, 'Truly this was the Son of God (Wahrlich,
dieser ist Gottes Sohn gewesen)', Bach has created perhaps the
two most impressive bars of music that can be found in his whole
output. He uses a double choir of voices and instruments in their
highest range, adds a strong dissonance in the organ part and
precedes the passage with a long, ominously low note on the
continuo instruments, the lowest possible, in fact. All this, together
with the sudden change of key which immediately precedes these
two bars, not only prepares the way for a very loud treatment
in order to realize the terror which has been dominant from the
first bar of the movement, but also suggests strongly that Bach
deliberately inflated these words (which may not even be translated correctly from the original, and were spoken only by a few
people) into a tremendous affirmation of faith. Treated thus, the
passage becomes the overwhelming climax to an overwhelming
work. (If these two bars are *not* treated loudly, a different kind
of climax to the work seems to me to come at the end of No.71.)

74(64).   Recitative, Bass, 'In the evening when it was cool (Am
Abend da es kühle war)'; free text; I strings and continuo

The first violins have continuous semiquavers based mainly on
a descending motif—perhaps symbolizing the descent from the
Cross—over a static bass, which latter imparts a very tranquil
mood to the whole piece. The middle parts provide the harmony
in gently swaying quavers. The total picture is one of relief and
relaxation, and as such is placed at a perfectly timed moment in
the work.

75(65).   Aria, Bass, 'Make thee clean, my heart (Mache dich,
mein Herze, rein)'; free text; I strings, oboe da caccia, and
continuo

Animated music returns with this twelve-eight movement, whose
gentle swing suggests something between a *Siciliana* and a *gigue*.
The music is full of subtle passages of imitation, not always easy
to hear; refreshing changes of metre occur at the cadences through
the use of hemiolic accents (see the discussion of No.32 in the St
John Passion for an explanation and another strong example of
this).

76(66a, b and c).   Recitative, Evangelist, Pilate and Chorus, 'And when Joseph had taken the body (Und Joseph nahm den Leib)'; tutti

In this account of what was done with Jesus's body, the 'rolling' shape of the music for 'rolled a great stone to the door of the sepulchre (wälzete einen grossen Stein vor die Tür des Grabes)' should not be missed (see Ex. 20). The start of the final crowd chorus (High Priests and Pharisees) is arresting, with the sopranos placed high: 'Sir [that is, Pilate], we remember that that deceiver said... After three days I will rise again [upward scales] (Herr, wir haben gedacht...)'; Pilate is certainly meant to hear and take notice, which he does, but throws the responsibility on to the Jews. The ending is angular, almost ugly, depicting 'the last error' (i.e. if Jesus were falsely said to have risen from the dead) being 'worse than the first' (i.e. the prophecy of resurrection).

Ex. 20: St Matthew No. 76

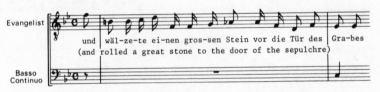

77(67).   Recitative, Soprano, Alto, Tenor, Bass and Chorus II, 'Now the Lord is laid to rest (Nun ist der Herr zur Ruh' gebracht)'; free texts; I strings and continuo, II flutes, oboes, strings and continuo

In the East close friends and relatives of a deceased person are traditionally each supposed to have spoken a final word at the graveside. Indeed, in the West a similar custom, though without spoken words, exists. This, at any rate, is what this beautiful movement is about. Again, there are two levels, the four soloists (I) making their individual remarks, and chorus II between each solo section singing a refrain 'My Jesus, farewell (Mein Jesu, gute Nacht)', but instruments of I imitate the 'My Jesus' motif of II as if unwilling to be left out. The interesting and important point here is that Bach was careful not to involve the whole world

of Christianity, namely the double chorus, but just the more
intimate circle of followers only slightly larger than that of the
eleven disciples.

78(68).   Double Chorus, 'We sit down with tears (Wir setzen
uns mit Tränen nieder)'; free text; tutti

The monumental final chorus is in the tradition of German
Passion closing choruses of the early eighteenth century, but this
example transcends all others, with the possible exception of that
in Bach's St John. The idea of bidding the Saviour rest peacefully
in the grave may be naïve, but it is attractive (see the discussion
of No.67 of the St John Passion in Chapter 5). The structural
basis of this chorus is that of a Sarabande (see Ex.21). The music

Ex. 21a: Sarabande from Suite in C minor, No. III of *Verschiedene
Instrumental-Kompositionen* (BG 45, II, p. 164)

Ex. 21b: after double bar, bar 17

which clothes it is magnificently strong; in the main section,
repeated at the end, the high held notes of the sopranos on 'call
(rufen)' always culminate in a crunching discord; they can, and
should, sound loud enough, one feels, to wake the dead! Which
seems to be what Bach had in mind, and is in keeping with all
the quasi-realistic and the mystical touches throughout both his
St Matthew and St John settings. The words 'rest softly' are

first *piano*, echoed *pianissimo*, and repeated *forte*. Terraced dynamics are also used in an exquisitely tender way at the end of the middle section on 'slumber (schlummern da die Augen ein)', where the sudden *piano* on 'schlummern' is reduced to *più piano* as the drooping phrases sink lower, and finally to *pianissimo* immediately before the return of the opening.

7

Changes Made by Bach in the St John and St Matthew Passions

The St John Passion underwent far more changes than did the St Matthew.[1] The first and last versions of the St John were the same as we know today except that in the first performance in 1724 No.61 was only three bars long. In the second performance in 1725, however, No.1 was replaced by the massive chorale fantasia on 'O Mensch, bewein' dein' Sünde gross' in the key of E flat, which we know in E major as the closing chorus of Part I of the St Matthew. Arthur Mendel, editor of the Neue Bach Ausgabe of the St John, believes that this movement originated earlier in Weimar, between 1714 and 1716.[2] In this same performance we find a bass aria 'Himmel reisse, Welt erbebe (Heavens tear asunder, earth tremble)' with a soprano chorale 'Jesu deine Passion (Jesu, thy Passion)', scored for two flutes and continuo, inserted between Nos.15 and 16, the tenor aria No.19 replaced by another tenor aria even more dramatic than the first, 'Zerschmettert mich, ihr Felsen und ihr Hügel (Crush me, oh ye hills and crags)', scored for strings, and a tenor aria 'Ach, windet euch nicht so, geplagte Seelen (Do not writhe so, oh ye tortured souls)' with two oboes and continuo, in the place of Nos.31 and 32. Finally, the closing chorale No.68 was supplanted by the chorale-chorus 'Christe du Lamm Gottes (Christ thou Lamm of God)', scored for tutti (two flutes, two oboes, strings and continuo). This is known to us as the final movement of Cantata No.23; according to surviving evidence its place in the Cantata just predates its appearance in the Passion.

Any assessment of the musical effect of these 1725 changes involves value-judgments of a personal character as well as a consideration of the overall effect from the dramatic and balance points of view. In general, there are musical gains from the substituted opening and closing numbers, magnificent as those in the original (i.e. the present) version are; the effect of 'Himmel

reisse, welt erbebe' after No.15 is to emphasize personal histrion-
ics in the manner of the Hamburg Passion poets; this number
is closely allied to Postel's 'Bebet, ihr Berge, berstet, ihr Hügel
(Tremble ye mountains, burst open ye hills)' from his St John
Passion, 1704, both in spirit and actual text. In Postel it comes
immediately after Jesus's death; in Bach, after Jesus has been
struck by one of the servants and a commenting chorale has been
sung. Postel has a similar aria after 'Crucify him', and Brockes
has one after the death. 'Zerschmettert mich' has similar sentiments to those of No.19 which it displaces, only they are more
dramatically expressed with sudden *Adagios* interrupting the
rushing downward scales which express the crushing hills and
crags. In the original aria the singer simply cries out 'Where
shall I go, where can I find comfort?' Here he knows what should
happen and calls on the hills to crush him, again in the manner
of the Hamburg Passions. The beautiful aria 'Ach, windet euch
nicht so' is nevertheless not quite up to the standard of the first
piece it displaces, the arioso No.31, 'Betrachte, meine Seel' ',
either in musical content or scoring, but the exchange with No.32,
'Erwäge', is a fair one. As far as the dramatic movement in Part
II of the whole work is concerned, the gain is considerable: we
get a needed commentary between the scourging (30) and Jesus
receiving the crown of thorns and purple robe (33), though it
lasts only about five minutes; in St John as we have it things are
held up for nearly a quarter of an hour at this point.

Which brings us to the first and last pieces in the work. For
the present writer Bach never wrote a more moving Passion
chorus than 'O Mensch, bewein' '; it is also likely to be more
successful in performance than 'Herr, unser Herrscher' which
contains so many balance problems for present-day musicians.
But to have two longish choruses—one of them in *Da Capo*
form—in succession at the close of the work as Bach did for the
second performance, is a distinct disadvantage. But 'Christe, du
Lamm Gottes', whose text is the *Agnus Dei*, is a rare and sublime
masterpiece, with its opening *Adagio* funeral march for section
I of the three-section text, and its lilting *Andante*, becoming
increasingly hopeful and finally triumphant in mood over the
last two sections. Certainly the closing chorale in the original
version contrasts the body lying dead in the grave with its final
resurrection in a telling and greatly comforting manner. But one

could say that it is unliturgical to contemplate thoughts relating
to Easter on Good Friday. Apart from its following the long
No.67, perhaps this *Agnus Dei* setting is therefore the ideal
ending, with its wonderful change to major tonality nine bars
from the end on 'peace' in 'Grant us thy peace' and the strong
Tierce de Picardy (major chord ending to a minor key piece) in
the final bar.

For his third performance of the St John Passion, probably
about 1730,[3] Bach deleted his borrowings from St Matthew's
Gospel, namely Peter's weeping at the end of No.18 and the
rending of the veil of the temple, the earthquake and so on, of
No.61. At the same time No.62 (which refers to these dramatic
events) and No.63 (whose opening is related thematically to the
end of No.62) were cut and, according to some of the orchestral
material, a sinfonia took their place, which has since been lost.[4]
In this performance Bach opened the work with the original first
movement 'Herr, unser Herrscher', but replaced 'Himmel, reisse'
by an aria now lost, deleted No.15 and reverted to the original
arioso No.31 and aria No.32 in place of the 'Ach, windet euch
nicht so' of 1725. The *Agnus Dei* ending was deleted.[5] This
version therefore had a great deal less solo vocal commentary
after Jesus's death (only Nos.60, 65 and the closing chorus) than
the other versions. The music of the fourth performance, towards
the end of Bach's life, was virtually as we know it today.

In order to get the changes which Bach made in the St John
Passion into perspective and to throw light on one or two aspects
of the St Matthew, one may state here that it is impossible to be
quite certain of the history and origin of some of the pieces in
both Passions. Scholars like Arthur Mendel and Alfred Dürr
have been working on the subject for many years.[6] Much is
conjectural owing, for example, to the lack of a complete autograph score of St John, existing autograph parts for instruments
which are not listed, and so on. In fact many movements may
have had quite early origins; this is sometimes suggested by the
orchestration, but has not been proved.

Similarly with the St Matthew Passion, there are several
theories suggesting an earlier date of composition than used to
be supposed. Certainly the earliest extant score made by Altnickol
about the end of the third decade of the eighteenth century was
itself a copy of the original manuscript (now lost) or possibly a

copy of that.[7] Furthermore, Dürr[8] supports the suggestion made by Smend that there may have been an earlier single-chorus St Matthew setting by Bach because the estate of his son Emanuel, who inherited much of his father's music, contained a list of the elder Bach's works, and this included a St Matthew Passion for double choir (the one we know) and another incomplete setting of the same Gospel. That some at least of a single chorus work may have been incorporated into the bigger work is suggested by the curious structure of the choruses in Nos.67 and 76, which begin antiphonally with two genuine four-part choruses, but soon lapse into four-part writing; an unusual thing for Bach to do.[9] Picander wrote a rhymed Passion libretto in 1725 and it has been pointed out that Nos.1, 25, 47, 58, 60 and 78 of Bach's St Matthew are based on this. Smend[10] supposes, among other matters relating to dating, that these numbers were therefore composed earlier than the rest of the work.

Altnickol's score formed the basis of the first performance of 1729. The principal differences between it and Bach's autograph score of (?) 1736 are as follows. In Altnickol's score, in No.1 the *ripieno* chorale 'O Lamm Gottes unschuldig' was 'not sung, but played on the little organ over the altar';[11] in No.12 it seems doubtful if flutes participated; No.35 consisted of a plainly harmonized chorale 'Jesum, lass' ich nicht von mir' in place of the fantasia 'O Mensch, bewein' '; in No.36 the soloist was a bass not an alto; and in Nos.65 and 66 the solo string instrument was a lute and not a gamba. Besides these changes for a performance in the 1730s, Bach made a further adjustment for one in the 1740s, when apparently a second organ was not available, introducing a gamba in Nos.40 and 41 to reinforce the substituting harpsichord continuo of Choir II. Except for the replacement of 'O Mensch, bewein' ', which obviously gives Part I a much better overall balance than the short chorale does, as well as being more in keeping with its emotional content, these changes are of a minor character and need no further comment.

8
Performances and Performance Styles

No direct information is available about the quality and standard of Bach's own performances of the Passions, nor about how they were received. But one can deduce something about the former from Bach's complaints to the Leipzig Town Council about the standard of his choir and orchestra (see Chapter 3). One imagines that at the beginning of his time in Leipzig, performances of the St John in 1724 and 1725 would have been better than that of the St Matthew in 1729, only eighteen months before his complaints about standards were made. Regarding the question of how the Passions were received, several points have to be considered in trying to form an opinion at this distance of time.

The style in which Bach wrote his mature works was becoming out of date before he died. He was out of touch with the new spirit of the time, for the Age of Reason was not in sympathy with the kind of religious texts which he set; simple tunes were preferred to complex counterpoint, simple textures to fugues and old-fashioned number symbolism. Number symbolism, a complicated and semi-mystical system of regarding numbers as having secret meanings and symbolizing pictures, aspects of the Deity and so on, was current from the Middle Ages until well into the eighteenth century. Adolph Scheibe, a Leipzig musician and journalist, was expressing the views of leading thinkers and also voicing the general feeling of the times when he wrote the following in his *Critical Musician* (1737).[1] Bach is not named but no-one will have doubted that it is he who was being attacked. Scheibe had been turned down for the post of organist at the Thomaskirche in 1729 and Bach was one of his examiners; Forkel, Bach's first biographer,[2] believed that Scheibe was avenging himself in this violent attack.

This great man would be the admiration of whole nations if he had more amenity, if he did not take away the natural elements in his pieces by giving them a turgid and confused style, and if he did not darken their beauty by an excess of art. . . Every ornament, every little grace, and everything that one thinks of as belonging to the method of playing, he expresses in notes; and this not only takes away from his pieces the beauty of harmony but completely covers the melody throughout. In short, he is in music what Mr von Lohenstein is in poetry. Turgidity has led them both from the natural to the artificial, and from the lofty to the sombre; and in both one admires the onerous labour and uncommon effort—which however are vainly employed, since they conflict with Reason.

One infers from this that Bach's Passions must have made little impression on most of the congregation, especially as even their form was unfamiliar (see Chapter 1). The following well-known comment, made by Bach's pupil H.N. Gerber in 1732, though now thought to apply to some event in Dresden, could well have applied to the Passions in Leipzig.

Some high officials and well-born ladies in one of the galleries began to sing the first Choral with great devotion from their books. But as the theatrical music proceeded, they were thrown into the greatest wonderment, saying to each other, 'What does it all mean?' While an old lady, a widow, exclaimed, 'God help us! 'tis surely an Opera-comedy!'[3]

During his twenty-seven years in Leipzig Bach seems to have been less revered as a composer than as a performer on the keyboard. Certain students, especially those in Berlin, and Rector Gesner were exceptions to this general attitude. We are indebted to his second son Emanuel for preserving many manuscripts and for making a collection of the chorales, but during his whole time as Cantor of the Johanneum and Director of Music in Hamburg's five principal churches, it never occurred to him to perform a single work of his father's. For a St Matthew Passion in 1769 he unscrupulously plundered his father's work and allowed the pastiche to go out under his own name.[4]

The first revival of Bach's St Matthew Passion after his death was exactly a hundred years after its first performance in 1729.* The St John had to wait even longer, until 1833, a hundred and nine years after it was originally heard.

*J. Rifkin[5] powerfully argues the case for accepting April 11, 1727 as the date of the first performance of the St Matthew, providing a mass of evidence. If this dating is correct, my emphasis and conclusions in regard to one or two matters discussed in this book will be slightly affected—notably the connection between the date of Bach's Memorandum to the Leipzig Town Council and its possible implications for the 'first' St Matthew performance (see page 17).

A group of Bach's pupils and their friends in Berlin kept his music alive by copying it out many times and distributing it during the second half of the eighteenth century, however, and lists of Cantatas and Motets in Breitkopf's catalogues in the 1760s suggest that they were commercially viable at this time. But it was through the Berlin circle that the music was eventually resurrected; two people were chiefly responsible. An Austrian diplomat, Baron van Swieten, joined the Bach circle when he served his term in Berlin. On his return to Vienna he held regular Sunday morning meetings in his house to study and play Bach's music; this is where Mozart first became acquainted with it; his famous first encounter with the Motets in Leipzig occurred seven years later (1789).

The first book about Bach and his music was written by Johann Nickolaus Forkel, who had studied with one of Bach's pupils, and became director of music at Göttingen University. It was published in 1802 and dedicated to van Swieten. The following words from the introduction show that it was in part the growth of German national consciousness that created the climate in which Bach's music could be appreciated: 'This great man, the greatest orator-poet who ever addressed the world in the language of music, was a German! Let Germany be proud of him. Yes, proud of him, but worthy of him too!' A clergyman in Stettin called Triest also apparently rehearsed and perhaps performed Bach's vocal works during the first half of the nineteenth century.[6] Whether these included Passions is not known. Triest apparently shared Forkel's views about the appeal Bach could have to the Germans who were beginning to become conscious of their national heritage.[7] Another factor in creating conditions favourable to the understanding of Bach was the changed attitude to religion, the swing away from the ideas of the Age of Reason towards a more religious attitude of life which occurred about the turn of the century.[8] Although Forkel's book disseminated knowledge of Bach, he himself was not in sympathy with the religious thought in the texts of the Passions and Cantatas, in fact he lists these works, but gives them no discussion at all.

Carl Friedrich Zelter, an important theorist and composer, founder of the Berlin Academy of Church and School Music, and Principal of the Berlin Singakademie, was the person through whom the first performance of the St Matthew Passion after Bach's death was brought about (he rehearsed the St John too, but the first performance took place after his decease). He had obtained a number of Bach's works through Kirnberger, Bach's most enthusiastic pupil, and Agricola, who with C.P.E. Bach wrote his funeral oration. The Singakademie, where Mendelssohn eventually revived the St Matthew Passion in 1829, was a society for the practice of music, especially sacred music. Founded in 1791, like the Berlin circle it was in a line of direct descent from Bach.

Zelter was the first person in Germany to acquire a real knowledge of Bach's vocal works, extending to the Passions and about a hundred Cantatas.[9] He did not believe it possible to perform these works in public because of the 'polemical earnestness of the Reformation contained in the chorales, and because of the music's complexity', and the difficulty of mustering the necessary forces; but in 1811 and 1813 he rehearsed the Mass in B Minor and in 1815 the St Matthew Passion. Zelter believed that the music should be stripped of its 'French froth' because Bach was 'a son of his age and could not escape the French influence',[10] a viewpoint of which his friend Goethe was highly critical. Zelter like Forkel did not fully understand the religious message of the Passions and Cantatas. But his enthusiasm for Bach's works as a whole greatly influenced the young Mendelssohn who was his student at the Singakademie, and enlarged the latter's already considerable knowledge. Mendelssohn had no sooner heard parts of the Passion rehearsed than he was determined to acquire a score of his own. Eventually Zelter gave permission for his score to be copied; this was done by the violinist Eduard Rietz (who later led the orchestra in Mendelssohn's performance) and it was presented to the fourteen-year-old Mendelssohn by his grandmother at Christmas 1823.[11]

Four years later Mendelssohn formed a small reliable choir for the purpose of rehearsing rare works. Very soon the St Matthew Passion was included in the rehearsal repertoire but there was still no thought of performing it. It was Eduard Devrient, an actor-singer student of Zelter's at the Singakademie, and close friend of Mendelssohn, who actually brought about the performance. He tells us that enthusiasm for the work had developed to a high point during rehearsals, and Mendelssohn had shown an extraordinary insight into the meaning of the music. Many of those who rehearsed it wished also to perform it, but were discouraged by the expectedly hostile attitude of the public brought up on performances of Graun's *Der Tod Jesu* ('The Death of Jesus')* on Good Fridays, and above all by Zelter's opposition.† Devrient however 'longed more and more ardently to sing the part of Christ in public'[13] and formed an inflexible determination to do so. All his friends were discouraging and 'the old ladies of the Akademie shook their heads.'[14] Mendelssohn himself made fun of the idea by offering to give a public performance of this unprecedentedly complex work on a rattle and penny trumpet.

Devrient, however, was not to be put off. Early one morning in January 1829, he went round to Mendelssohn's house, had him dragged out of bed, and told him of his intention to perform the Passion that season, and of his determination that Mendelssohn would conduct. Mendelssohn protested his inadequacy for such a task, but eventually agreed. Together they went to put the idea to Zelter. Although Devrient delivered a carefully prepared speech, Zelter was irritated and discouraged them by putting up many obstacles, such as the large resources needed and the lack of experience of two such 'young donkeys' as Devrient and Mendelssohn. Indeed the latter was for giving up, but Devrient continued his argument by saying that it would reflect as much credit on Zelter himself as on them if two of his pupils could bring off this great result. This made Zelter relent, though grudgingly, uttering such remarks as 'You will have nothing but misery... Today ten will come to rehearsal, tomorrow, twenty will stop away.'[15] But after this everything went smoothly; indeed the numbers attending rehearsals increased on every occasion, so that the copyist could hardly keep up with demands; at the performance the chorus consisted of 47 sopranos, 36 altos, 34 tenors and 41 basses.

---

*This work, first performed in 1755, had an immense vogue over many years. It contains a good deal of imaginative music, but it was more a Cantata based loosely on sentiments engendered by the Passion story than a liturgical Passion. It fails even to give any specific account of the trial and death of Jesus.

†It should be mentioned that the accuracy of some aspects of Devrient's story, especially its references to Zelter's attitude, has been questioned by some Berlin musicians closely connected with the Singakademie.[12]

The exact size and constitution of the orchestra is difficult to ascertain, but it included some of the finest players in the city.[16] One source says that clarinets were substituted for oboi da caccia. 'And to think', said Mendelssohn triumphantly one day, standing still in the middle of the Opernplatz, 'that it should be an actor and a Jew that give back to the people the greatest of Christian works.'

It was decided that the work must be cut because so much of it was written in 'an old style' that would be incomprehensible. Most of the arias were omitted and of others only the instrumental sections given. The part of the Evangelist was stripped of all that was not essential. There was no difficulty in getting solo singers: four of the chief Singakademie opera singers were, as Devrient relates,

ready and willing to help us. Their participation in the rehearsals, and the greater finish these now assumed, gave a fresh impetus to our work. Musicians and amateurs all thronged to the rehearsals, anxious to understand it better and better. All were amazed, not only at its architectonic grandeur of structure, but at its abundance of melody, its wealth of expression and of passion, at its quaint and affecting declamation, and at its dramatic power. No one had ever suspected old Bach of all this.

But Felix's share in making the splendid properties of this work felt and known is as memorable as the undertaking itself. His perfect mastery of all its details was only half his merit. His energy, perseverance, tact, and clever calculation of the resources at hand, made this masterpiece modern, intelligible, and life-like once more... The revered presence of Zelter gave still greater importance to the orchestral rehearsals. Until these took place, Felix had both to accompany and to conduct, a difficult matter with the rapid alternations of chorus and solos in ever-changing rhythms: here he used to play the accompaniment with the left hand, and conduct with the right.

When we had an orchestra, the piano [from which Mendelssohn conducted, according to his sister Fanny][17] was placed across the platform, between the two choirs; it was then not yet customary for the conductor to turn his back to the audience, except at the opera. By this means, though the first choir was behind Felix, he faced the second and the orchestra. This latter consisted mainly of amateurs [cf. pages 17-18 re Bach's forces]; only the leaders of the string and principal wind instruments belonged to the royal chapel. The wind instruments were placed at the back, above the semicircular platform, and extended towards the small concert-room through three open doors. The task of keeping steady this waving mass devolved upon Eduard Rietz.

Felix was as calm and collected in his difficult post as though he had already conducted a dozen Festivals. The quiet and simple way in which he, by a look, a movement of the head or hand, reminded us of the inflections agreed upon, and thus ruled every phrase...[18]

In his autobiography published in 1896, Sir Charles Hallé, who met Mendelssohn in Frankfurt in 1841, states an astonishing thing about the historic performance. Mendelssohn, he writes, 'found, stepping to the conductor's desk, that a score similar in binding and thickness, but of another work, had been brought by mistake. He conducted the amazingly complicated work by heart, turning leaf after leaf of the book he had before him, in order not to create any feeling of uneasiness on the part of the executants.'

Of the performance itself, on 11 March 1829, Devrient tells us that the ladies interpreted their solo parts expressively with good voice, that the Evangelist (Stümer) sang 'with quiet precision... and without expatiating on the pathetic passages in the second part;'[19] and of his own singing of the part of Christ and the general effect of the whole performance he writes:

Deeply affected by the work as it proceeded, I sang with my whole soul and voice and believed that the thrills of devotion that ran through my veins were also felt by the rapt hearers. Never have I known any performance so consecrated by one united sympathy.

Our Concert made an extraordinary sensation in the educated circles of Berlin. This repopularizing of a half-forgotten master was felt to be of pregnant import. A second performance was called for, which took place on 21st March, and was crowded like the first. There was yet one more, under Zelter, after Felix's departure, on Good Friday, 17 April, in lieu of the usual 'Tod Jesu' of Graun.[20]

Devrient told Mendelssohn in a letter that Zelter's was a 'feeble' performance.[21] The impression Mendelssohn received from this letter was that the effect of the Passion performances had soon worn off.

J. Theodor Mosevius, founder and conductor of the Singakademie in Breslau, was present at Mendelssohn's performance, and gave the work himself in Breslau in 1830. Blume[22] states that Mosevius developed more understanding of the mind and spirit of Bach than did Zelter or Mendelssohn, and that the Bach movement he led in Breslau included the performances of many Cantatas. On the other hand, a performance in Königsberg in 1832 was unsuccessful because of a lack of 'religious background'; indeed 'some of the congregation ran out of the church even during the first half'. Others criticized the work as '"out of date rubbish"'.[23] The first performance of the St Matthew Passion in Leipzig after Bach's death took place in 1841.

The comment 'out of date rubbish' is understandable, for even Zelter, Mendelssohn and Mosevius did not fully understand Bach's style. In general they respected the score, although Mendelssohn added more instruments in No. 73 of the St Matthew, despite the fact that Bach's own scoring for bass strings and organ only is enormously effective in suggesting the noise of the tearing of the veil of the temple. Mozart had set a fashion in writing 'additional accompaniments' to several Handel works (his *Messiah* accompaniments were in general use until quite recently) and the misunderstanding of the late baroque timbres and textures which began soon after the style declined in the mid-eighteenth century led to a series of Bach 'arrangements' in the nineteenth century which persisted into the twentieth. Indeed the use of these rescorings by conductors lasted until well after the Second World War. The most popular orchestral rescoring of the St Matthew Passion was that of Robert Franz (1815–92)[24] who also arranged in a similar manner Bach's Magnificat and ten of the Cantatas. Undoubtedly these arrangements helped to popularize the works concerned.

One of the most extreme German 'improvers' of Bach was Dr Heinrich Reimann, whose score of the St John Passion (1903) had additional parts for clarinets, contra-bassoon, horns, trumpets, trombones, timpani and bass drum; the Chorales, scored for *tutti* without percussion, must have sounded atrocious, but some effects, like the timpani entry six and a half bars from the end of 'Crucify' (No.36) and the bass drum rolls in the veil of the temple/earthquake recitative (No.61), could have made an exciting effect.

The first performance of St John after Bach's death took place in 1833 at the Berlin Singakademie and was directed by Carl Friedrich Rungenhagen, Zelter's successor as Principal, but during the nineteenth century it was comparatively neglected.

Naturally, an important influence on nineteenth-century performances was the publication of the scores. St Matthew appeared in 1830, St John in 1831. In 1850 the Bach Gesellschaft was founded, to publish the entire works of Bach in a scholarly edition.

The style of presentation of the Passions during the century and a quarter following Mendelssohn's performance in 1829 did not change much in its basic approach. Enthusiasm and devotion were not lacking, but in the light of what the Bach Gesellschaft scores which were available during the latter half of the century revealed, and what we now know about early eighteenth-century performance practice, ignorant, misguided attitudes persisted for a surprisingly long time.

Albert Schweitzer had practical experience of Passion performances in France and Germany around the turn of the century. He complains bitterly about their style in his book on Bach. He criticizes most the enormous size of choirs, which made clarity of texture and audibility of the orchestra difficult or almost impossible to achieve. Other points to be learnt from Schweitzer about Bach performance style at this time are that instrumental phrasing and accentuation were unmusical and unintelligent respectively, despite 'correct' bowing and fingering; that slowing up at every cadence was too often indulged in by singers, with a resulting bad ensemble; that the singing of recitatives suffered in a similar way, and they were furthermore treated far too slowly and romantically to make sense, especially in Passion narratives, where the Evangelist would 'depict' the events described, instead of just telling the story; that there was no uniformity in the matter of trilling (nor is there today, especially in Germany!); that the notes which should be 'realized' on the organ from the figured bass part were totally ignored, with atrocious results to the music's texture, such as reducing it to two parts, perhaps a soprano voice and a bass instrument with a yawning gap of two or three octaves between them.

The misunderstanding of the keyboard continuo part, that is, the belief that it was not essential, and the huge size of choirs were two reasons for the practice of scoring for additional instruments during the nineteenth century.

Schweitzer's plea for the revival of period instruments like the viola d'amore and the viola da gamba and the clear, bright-toned baroque organ confirms that these instruments were not available in the nineteenth and early twentieth centuries. In 1904 Max Seiffert[25] argued that if practical experiments with using period instruments were made, we should decide against them. His realization of the figured continuo part, although paying scant respect to the harmonies indicated by Bach, made possible something like a correct treatment to be made of the orchestral texture in the Passions and Cantatas at a time when the art of playing from figured bass seems to have largely died out. In the first vocal (piano) score of the St Matthew Passion (1830) none of the harmony notes indicated by Bach's figuring appears in the 'accompaniment', only the orchestral parts. Schweitzer suggests, with a touch of ironical humor, that conductors cut those movements the stark and empty *look* of which they found 'unendurable'!

Schweitzer made impassioned pleas in 1905 for the use of boys' voices, a suitable organ sound and the realization of the continuo without additional instruments. Boys have only begun to be used for Bach outside cathedrals and large churches since the late 1960s and early '70s, the 'baroque' organ reproductions since about twenty years earlier, and as recently as 1956 the present writer heard performances at the Ansbach Bach Festival at which the conductor, directing from the keyboard, omitted the continuo realization in the first few bars of every movement while he was getting it started from a standing position; from which one infers that it was still not regarded as essential.

Not until a decade or so after the Second World War did Passion performances in Europe begin to take on an authentic scale or style, and then only in limited areas. Nevertheless the 'romantic' versions of the Passions given, for example, by Mengelberg (Holland) between the wars and Gunter Ramin (Leipzig) were memorable for their warmth and sincerity.

In recent times, historical awareness has been shown by only comparatively few groups, and at the time of writing the most popular performances and recordings of the Passions in Germany still tend towards the romantic style of the nineteenth century rather than the style of the early eighteenth century. The South (Munich) is characterized by a heavy nineteenth-century approach, which often ignores both specific and implied directions in the score; in the centre (Stuttgart) the style is less heavy, and more musical, but all the playing and singing is monotonously legato (a tendency that in part arose in reaction against the over-staccato singing prevalent in South Germany during the 1950s). A famous group from Hamburg, visiting the English Bach Festival in the late 1960s, showed scant respect for the St Matthew Passion's antiphonal writing by doubling the two groups in several numbers in which they should be separate. At the time of writing it is only in Austria (Vienna) and Holland that performances are being given and recordings made combining 'period' instruments, all-male choirs, and stylistic ornamentation and rhythm, albeit at some expense in interpretation.

The foundations for a Bach cult in America were laid when eighteenth-century settlers from Moravia, Bohemia and Saxony arrived in Pennsylvania about 1741. These people of German stock, many from the area where Bach worked, put down their roots in and around Bethlehem, Pennsylvania, which became the headquarters of a 'zealous, evangelizing church'.[26] The Moravians brought their musical tradition from Europe and in 1754 a quartet of trombones played at the Sunrise Easter Service. From 1744 until 1820 a Collegium Musicum of Moravian singers and instrumentalists gave regular concerts of music by the great composers of Europe.[27] Benjamin Franklin and George Washington testified to the excellence of the performances.[28] In 1820 the Collegium was reformed as a Philharmonic Society.

The Choral Union was founded in 1880; in 1885 its director, Dr J. Fred Wolle, heard the St John Passion given in Munich by a large choir on the occasion of the two hundredth anniversary of Bach's birth. He went back 'bent on converting to Bach the members of his Bethlehem Choral Union'.[29] Three years later, on June 5, 1888, he gave the St John Passion complete[30] using a choir of 115 singers. It was four years before Wolle could persuade his choir to tackle the more difficult St Matthew Passion, but in 1892 the work was given complete for the first time. After this the Choral Union passed out of existence and a Bach Choir was formed.

In 1900 the first Bach Festival took place. A second Festival took place in 1901; the *New York Times* reviewer referred to 'a performance in which the sublimity of the music was perfectly disclosed.' Festivals continued yearly at Bethlehem until 1905; then Wolle took the Chair of Music at the University of California in Berkeley. There he gave the Mass in B minor and the St Matthew Passion in 1909 and 1910. After six years he returned to Bethlehem and continued conducting Bach Festivals from 1912 with a reorganized Bach Choir of 250–300 voices until 1932. Dr Wolle died in 1933.

In his manner of performance, Wolle was against sensationalism and any form of personal aggrandisement (he forbade his name to appear on programmes), but he seized every chance of making the music expressive and bringing out the pictorial elements in it. To obtain maximum expressiveness he used no baton, only his fingers. Wolle was succeeded by Bruce Carey and, in 1939, by Ifor Jones, a Welshman trained in England. The scale of performances during this period continued to be large: 'nearly three hundred voices and an orchestra of ninety' (the Philadelphia Symphony) are mentioned in 1935.[31]

The Bethlehem concerts of Bach Passions were not the first performances in America. A shortened version of the St John had been given by the Boston Handel and Haydn Society in the 1870s and the New York Oratorio Society had presented the St Matthew in 1880.

Bach Cantata Clubs sprang up after the First World War, based on the English model directed by Kennedy Scott (see below) and Bach Festivals, all deriving from Bethlehem's pioneering example, became established in Carmel, California, Berea, Ohio and Philadelphia.

Many choral directors in America are today wary of tackling the Passions because of the controversy which rages round the question of what is the correct performance practice of the period. Men like Julius Herford and Robert Shaw have done sterling work in encouraging stylish Bach, the former chiefly through workshops and lectures, the latter through practical example with his Robert Shaw Chorale, which has toured Bach all over America many times. Outside universities and church circles, Passion performances are given in big centres—but as elsewhere in the world, including the country of Bach, they can be woefully romantic and lacking in understanding of the music's spirit, style and scale.

Samuel Wesley was the driving force which brought knowledge of Bach's music to Britain in the early nineteenth century. He was fanatically enthusiastic, as can be seen from his Bach Letters written in 1808 and 1809,[32] and on 3 June 1809 introduced one of the Motets, 'Jesu meine Freude', at a 'Morning Musical Party' at the Hanover Square Rooms.[33] This was the first performance of any Bach choral work in Britain. Wesley and Mendelssohn were friends, chiefly through their common interest in Bach. The former had been conductor of the Birmingham Festival and therefore had some influence on its choice of programmes. Mendelssohn directed his St Paul there in 1837 and also played Bach's great Organ Prelude and Fugue in E flat. Between them Wesley and Mendelssohn persuaded the authorities to include the duet No.33 from the St Matthew Passion in the programme; this was eight years after it had first been heard in Berlin. However, the performance was evidently bad, for the piece was criticized in the *Birmingham Gazette* as 'a laboured production, unvocal and unfit for the words'.[34] But it seems to have made a fair impression in some quarters, for representatives of the London Choral Harmonists' Society and possibly Lord Burghersh (later Earl of Westmorland and founder of the Royal Academy of Music) were present, and the Magnificat and parts of the 'First Grand Mass' (?B minor Mass) were put on in London the following year. Nos.1, 2 and 11 of the Magnificat were 'well scored by Mr Kearns'; in other words, Mr Kearns (a minor composer and arranger) added to, and tried, in his ignorance, to improve Bach's score.

On 17 October 1849 the Bach Society (of London) was founded to work for 'the collection of the musical works' and 'the furtherance and promotion of a general acquaintance with the numerous vocal works... chiefly by performance'. The composer Sterndale Bennett was elected its first president. He directed what is claimed to have been the first performance of the St Matthew Passion in Britain at the Hanover Square Rooms on 6 April 1854, though the New Philharmonic Society had presented a very short selection from it two weeks earlier in St Martin's Hall.

Sir John Stainer, later recalling rehearsals for Bennett's St Matthew performance which he attended when a boy of nine, says that one Hogarth[35] said to the conductor, 'Mr Bennett, couldn't we have a little expression in the chorales?' to which Bennett replied 'Oh! Yes, by all means; there are none in the original, but I see no objection to some being introduced.' Stainer believed that this was the origin of expression marks in the chorales, and it could imply that Mendelssohn put no expression marks in his copy, though this seems unlikely (in this Bach Society performance some of the actual vocal parts—all in manuscript—which Mendelssohn had used in 1829 at Berlin were sent over to Bennett, probably for his guidance in preparing the work).[36] Bennett repeated the Passion later the same year and again in 1858 when the Prince Consort was present.

Of the St Martin's Hall performance the *Musical Times* reviewer was 'happy to say, considering the peculiarity of the style' that it was 'received with much favour';[37] of the more important performance by the Bach Society, the reviewer of the *Illustrated London News* of 25 April 1854 wrote: 'the Passionsmusik failed to produce the expected effect; it was found dry and heavy, and was very coldly received. Bach is a great and time-honoured name; but his vocal music is very little known in England, and what is known hardly seems to justify the veneration of his classical admirers.'[38]

In 1862 the Bach Society published by subscription the first English vocal score of the St Matthew Passion, edited by Sterndale Bennett and with a good translation by Helen Johnston.

The next landmark in the history of English Bach Passion concerts was Sir Joseph Barnby's nearly complete performance in Exeter Hall, London on 6 April 1870 with his Oratorio Concerts Choir, five hundred strong. Sir Joseph Barnby (born 1838) was an organist and composer (famous for 'Sweet and Low') but better known as a fine choir trainer. The 'thunder and lightning' chorus made an 'overwhelming effect' and was encored, and spontaneous applause was also bestowed on the chorales, 'sung with a decision and pathos which we have never heard before'. But it seems strange today to read that the audience 'deserved praise' for the attention it gave to the recitatives and to the final chorus ('usually a signal for a general rising').[39] Barnby repeated the St Matthew in 1871, and then formed a male choir to give it in the Abbey on Maundy Thursday (1871), the first performance recorded in England in a consecrated building. In 1873 Barnby gave three performances in the Albert

Hall and one each in St Paul's and the Abbey. In the Albert Hall the following year the audience took part in the chorales and were assisted by cornet players 'stationed at the several entrances to the audience-part of the hall', books of chorale words with melodies being sold at a nominal charge.[40]

The first performance in Britain of the St John was given by Barnby at the Hanover Square Rooms in March 1872. The *Musical Standard* reviewer was non-committal about the quality of the work at a first hearing, but thought it was 'in no way inferior' to the St Matthew.[41] *The Musical Times* critic complained of the organ (as opposed to the piano in current St Matthew performances) sustaining too much in recitatives. One hundred and five years later we are still complaining of it in most German performances!

Barnby did much to spread the gospel of Bach's Passion music, one of the most important results being the creation of a Bach cultural centre at St Anne's, Soho, with annual performances of the St John Passion with a comparatively small church choir (sixty-one for a Cantata in 1875).

Selections from the St Matthew Passion soon began to figure in special musical services: for instance in Westminster Abbey in 1872, in one which was attended by 3,000 people, 'the lovely unaccompanied chorales produced the finest effect'. The final sentence of the *Musical Standard*'s review is significant and must be quoted: 'The want of accord in pitch between different instruments sadly illustrates the necessity for some recognized and fixed English standard.'[42]

It is tempting to delve further into Victorian and Edwardian performances, for there were many, and reports of them throw interesting light on general attitudes to music at the time, but we must now turn to the 1920s and the work of Charles Kennedy Scott and his friends and supporters.

Scott, who devoted much of his life to promoting English music, fought for the restoration of the authentic small choir in Bach, and for this purpose the Bach Cantata Club was founded by his friend Hubert Foss in 1926. It had a chorus of about 30. At a performance of the St John Passion on 23 February 1932 the choir (actually numbering 31) was semi-professional, in that only the men were paid. A chamber orchestra was led by George

Stratton (one-time leader of the London Symphony Orchestra). Top professional singers sang the solos.

Harold Darke, for many years organist of St Michael's, Cornhill in the City of London, worked on similar lines at about the same time with his St Michael's Singers, who gave the St John regularly at Cornhill, and sometimes held Bach Festivals, performing on a bigger scale in such churches as St Margaret's, Westminster.

The Bach Choir, founded in 1876 to perform the Mass in B minor, established annual performances of the St Matthew Passion with a choir of between three and four hundred voices on Passion Sunday from 1894. Between the wars annual performances of St Matthew were given in Southwark Cathedral under Dr Cook, and many provincial cathedrals also gave regular performances of the Passions, most often St Matthew.

The following statistics are illuminating: during the 1886–7 season there was one performance of each Passion in Britain; during the 1926–7 season there were eight St Matthews and three St Johns.[43]

During the first forty years or so of the twentieth century Henry Wood popularized Bach's works, including the Passions; the orchestral parts he used are meticulously marked, for he left nothing to chance. Remarks about the mood and meaning of the words and music which are scattered plentifully throughout his scores reveal an insight not always evident in fashionably slick performances of today. To underline what he felt was in the music he added to the scoring. For example, in St Matthew he muted the string accompaniment to Jesus; in the cry from the cross 'My God, my God, why hast thou forsaken me?' (No.71) he had the poignant organ harmonies written out for strings and marked *vibrato*, muted and *ppp*; the veil of the temple/earthquake recitative (No.73) he fully scored for strings *tremolando*, and in the following two-bar chorus 'Truly this was the Son of God', evidently meant to be sung in an awe-struck *pianissimo*, he had half the first violins playing the soprano part an octave higher *ppp*; and he added flutes and oboes to some string *ritornelli* (e.g. No.61). At a time when the original orchestration of Bach's and Handel's works had scarcely been heard of, Wood's version must have made a considerable impact. The present writer, when a student, heard Sir Henry say in a lecture that if he was giving a performance of a Passion, what he studied first was the story in the Gospel.

At the Leith Hill Festival Vaughan Williams directed over many years a unique version of the St Matthew Passion; unique in that he wrote out a full continuo part for piano and organ (he couldn't stand the harpsichord), slightly re-ordered some of the movements, scored the oboi da caccia parts for solo violas because he disliked the intonation of the cor anglais of those days, used piccolos and quadrupled the flutes to get a satisfactory balance with a large choir.

After the Second World War Kennedy Scott's and Harold Darke's were the only small choirs in London outside cathedrals performing the Passions until the London Bach Society (sixty singers) was formed by the present writer in 1947. Apart from the emphasis on what in 1947 was regarded as a small number of singers, the Society began in 1950 to sing the works of Bach in German, and in 1952 gave the first public performance in Britain of the St Matthew Passion complete and in the original language in the Priory Church of St Bartholomew-the-Great, Smithfield. The performance was very well received and although the language caused controversy at first, the work has been repeated annually ever since. With the help of the late Bach scholar Walter Emery, this performance corrected a number of textural inaccuracies current at the time.

During the late 1960s and '70s a genuine historical awareness as regards style in Bach performances has grown up in Britain, gradually at first, but since the early '70s arguably too rapidly for the technical proficiency of players to keep pace, or rather, for them to be able to cope adequately in the shortage of rehearsal time in which, unfortunately, they have to work.

The trend towards the 'authentic' should be two-pronged, that is to say it should concern both the vocal and the instrumental sound, as it does, for example, with the Concentus Musicus in Vienna. But at the time of writing, very little attention has been given outside Vienna to the quality of soloists' tone or the constitution, tone and size of choirs. Another matter which has not yet had much attention in the hot pursuit of authenticity is the effect of the modern heating of buildings, particularly on instruments. Moreover, the sound of baroque instruments in Leipzig and of those, for example, in Paris or Naples was different, but only a very few specialists show practical care over this, or about the precise dates of instruments used.

Fortunately, performances of the Passions in Britain offer a wide variety of styles and scales. Between the extremes of a mammoth chorus and the all-male choirs and baroque instruments of the 'Back to Bach' movement there are many fine performances in churches, cathedrals and universities' public halls which are stylish without being rigidly didactic in approach. German is now the usual language in London but English versions are usually heard elsewhere. At present Britain probably offers better examples of middle-of-the-road style of performance than any other country.

Origins of Words and Melodies of the Chorales in Bach's Passions[1]

St John Passion

No. 7   Words: Verse seven of 'Herzliebster Jesu (O blessed Jesu)' by Johann Heerman (1585–1647); published in Leipzig, 1630.
Melody: 'Herzliebster Jesu' by Johann Cruger (1598–1662); published 1640 in Berlin.

No. 9   Words: Verse four of a versification of the Lord's Prayer by Martin Luther (1483–1546).
Melody: 'Vater unser im Himmelreich (Our Father, which art in Heaven)'; composer anonymous (?Luther). Words and music published 1539 in Leipzig.

No.15   Words: Verses three and four of 'O Welt, sieh' hier dein Leben (Oh World, behold here thy Life' by Paul Gerhardt (1607–76), published 1647 in Berlin.
Melody: 'O Welt, ich muss dich lassen (Oh World, I must leave thee)' by Heinrich Isaak (born c.1440); published originally to

Ex. 22: 'O Welt, ich muss dich lassen'   H. Isaak 1539

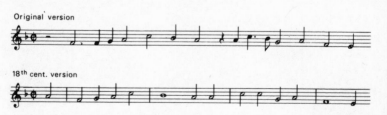

Original version

18th cent. version

secular words: 'Innsbruck, I now must leave thee' in Nürnberg in 1539, later associated with the words 'O Welt, ich muss dich lassen' and published by J. Hesse in Nürnberg, c.1555.

No.20   Words: Verse ten of 'Jesu Leiden, Pein und Tod (Jesu suffering pain and death)' by Paul Stockmann (?1602–36); published 1633 in Leipzig.
Melody: 'Jesu Kreuz, Leiden und Pein (Jesu cross, suffering and pain)' by Melchior Vulpius (c.1566–1615); published 1609 in Jena.

Ex. 23: 'Jesu Kreuz, Leiden und Pein'   M. Vulpius 1609

No.21   Words: a free translation of the Latin hymn 'Patris sapientia, veritas divina' by Michael Weisse (?1480–1534); published 1531 in Bohemia.
Melody: That which was proper to the Latin hymn and published with the words by Weisse in 1531, but Bach uses Calvisius's version of it as a basis, published 1598 in Leipzig.

No.27   Words: Verses eight and nine of 'Herzliebster Jesu'.
Melody: 'Herzliebster Jesu'.
For full details see No.7 above.

No.40   Words: Unknown author, or C.F. Postel of Hamburg, 1704 (see below).
Melody: 'Mach's mit mir Gott, nach deiner Gut (Be mindful of me, O God, after Thy Goodness); published with words of the same title by J.H. Schein (1586–1630), one of Bach's predecessors at the Thomaskirche, Leipzig, in that city in 1628.

Ex. 24: 'Mach's mit mir'   J.H. Schein 1628

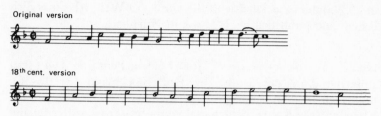

Original version

18th cent. version

In the St John Passion text of 1704 by Postel of Hamburg, this stanza occurs at precisely the same point in the narrative (see Chapter 5 for details of its treatment). C.S. Terry, in his book on Bach's Passions, written later than that on the Chorales, attributes the words to Postel.

No.52   Words: Verse three of 'Valet will ich dir geben... (Farewell I give thee, O World)', a hymn for the dying by Valerius Herberger (1562–1627); written during the Silesian Plague in 1613 and published in Leipzig in 1614.
Melody: 'Valet will ich dir geben' by Melchior Teschner (1584–1635); published with the words in 1614 in Leipzig.

No.56   Words: Verse twenty of 'Jesu Leiden, Pein und Tod'.
Melody: 'Jesu Kreuz, Leiden und Pein'. For details see No.20 above.

No.60   Words: Verse thirty-four of 'Jesu Leiden, Pein und Tod'.
Melody: 'Jesu Kreuz, Leiden und Pein'.
For details see No.20 above.

No.65   Words: Verse eight of 'Christus, der uns selig macht'.
Melody: 'Christus, der uns selig macht'.
For details see No.21 above.

No.68   Words: Verse three of 'Herzlich Lieb' hab' ich dich (Heartfelt love have I for thee)', a hymn for the dying by Martin Schalling (1532–1608); published in Nürnberg in 1571.
Melody: 'Herzlich Lieb' hab' ich dich', anonymous; published in 1577 in Strassburg.

Ex. 25: 'Herzlich Lieb' hab' ich dich, O Herr'   Anon. 1577

Original version

18th cent. version

St Matthew Passion

No.1 (*Ripieno* chorale) Verse one of 'O Lamm Gottes unschuldig (O guiltless Lamb of God)', a translation of the *Agnus Dei, qui tollis peccata mundi* by Nicolaus Decius (d.1541); published 1531 in Rostock in low German and 1539 in Leipzig in high German.
Melody: 'O Lamm Gottes unschuldig' composed or adapted by Decius; published with the hymn in Erfurt in 1542.

Ex. 26: 'O Lamm Gottes unschuldig'   N. Decius 1542

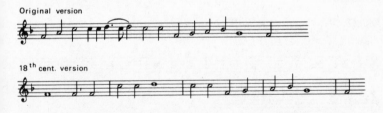

Original version

18th cent. version

No.3   Words: Verse one of 'Herzliebster Jesu'.
Melody: 'Herzliebster Jesu'.
For details see St John, No.7.

No.16   Words: Verse five of 'O Welt, sieh' hier dein Leben'.
Melody: 'O Welt ich muss dich lassen'.
For details see St John, No.15.

No.21 Words: Verse five of 'O Haupt voll Blut (Oh head, full of blood)', a translation of *Salve caput cruentatum* (St Bernard of Clairvaulx) by Paul Gerhardt (1607–76); published in 1656 in Frankfurt.
Melody: 'Herzlich thut mich verlangen (My heart is filled with longing)' by Hans Leo Hassler, who originally composed it for the secular song 'Mein G'mut ist mir verwirret von einer Jungfrau zart (My heart is troubled by a tender maiden)'; attached to the hymn whose name it now bears, it was published in 1613 in Görlitz.

No.23 Words: Verse six of 'O Haupt voll Blut'.
Melody: 'Herzlich thut mich verlangen'.
For details see No.21 above.

No.25 Words: Verse three of 'Herzliebster Jesu'.
Melody: 'Herzliebster Jesu'.
For details see St John, No.7.

No.31 Words: 'Was mein Gott will (What my God wills)' by Albrecht, Margrave of Brandenburg-Culmbach (1522–57); published in Nürnberg in 1554.
Melody: 'Was mein Gott will' from the anonymous French melody 'Il me souffit de tous mes maux' published in Paris in 1529. It first appeared attached to the present hymn in Erfurt in 1572.

Ex. 27: 'Was mein Gott will'   Anon. 1572

No.35 Words: Verse one of 'O Mensch, bewein' dein' Sünde gross (O Man, bewail thy grievous sin)' by Sebald Heyden (d.1561); published in Nürnberg in 1525.

Melody: 'Es sind doch selig alle (All are surely blessed)' by Matthias Greitter (c.1490–1550); published in Strassburg in 1525.

No.38   Words: Verse five of 'In dich hab' ich gehoffet (In Thee have I hoped)' by Adam Reissner (or Reusner) (1496–1575); published in Augsburg in 1533.
Melody: 'In dich hab' ich gehoffet' by Seth Calvisius (1556–1615), one of Bach's predecessors at Leipzig; published in Nürnberg in 1581.

No.44   Words: Verse three of 'O Welt, sieh' hier dein Leben'.
Melody: 'O Welt ich muss dich lassen'.
For details see St John, No.15.

No.48   Words: Verse six of 'Werde munter, mein Gemüthe (Be happy, my soul)' by Johann Rist (1607–1667); published in Lüneburg in 1642.
Melody: 'Werde munter, mein Gemüthe' by Johann Schop (d.c.1665); published with the words in Lüneberg in 1642.

No.53   Words: Verse one of 'Befiehl du deine Wege (Commend thou thy ways)' by Paul Gerhardt (1607–76); published in Frankfurt in 1656.
Melody: 'Herzlich thut mich verlangen'.
For details see No.21 above.

No.63   Words: Verses one and two of 'O Haupt voll Blut'.
Melody: 'Herzlich thut mich verlangen'.
For details see No.21 above.

No.72   Words: Verse nine of 'O Haupt voll Blut'.
Melody: 'Herzlich thut mich verlangen'.
For details see No.21 above.

Notes

See Bibliography for full details of references (which are to first-mentioned editions)

1: THE GERMAN PASSION TRADITION BEFORE BACH

1 Johann Matthias Gesner, Latin commentary to Marcus Fabius Quintilianus, *Institutiones Oratoriae*, 1738, quoted in David and Mendel, p.231.
2 Eton Choir MS, No.178; see Grove, *Dictionary of Music and Musicians*, edited by M. Blom, London, 1954, II, p.616.
3 See *The Collected Works of William Byrd*, edited Fellowes, London, 1938, V, pp.198–206.
4 *Historia der Passion und Leidens unsers einigen Erlösers... Jesu Christi*, Kassel, 1960.
5 *Passion nach dem Evangelisten Johannes... Das Chorwerk* XXVII, Wolfenbüttel and Berlin, 1934.
6 *Das Chorwerk* XXVI, Wolfenbüttel and Berlin, 1934.
7 *Denkmäler deutscher Tonkunst* XVII, Leipzig, 1904.
8 *Denkmäler deutscher Tonkunst* XVII, Leipzig, 1904.
9 *Matthäus Passion. Das Chorwerk* LXXVIII–LXXIX, Wolfenbüttel, 1961.
10 David and Mendel, p.90.
11 Edited by P. Steinitz, Oxford University Press, London, 1961.
12 Blume, 1975, p.251.
13 Ibid., p.254.
14 Quoted in David and Mendel, p.120—see Chapter 3, page 18 for a further quotation.
15 But see Geiringer, p.328.

2: THE BAROQUE STYLE OF COMPOSITION

1 The best is probably Donington.
2 See A. Harman and A. Milner, *Late Renaissance and Baroque Music*, London, 1959, p.201.

3 See *Musical Times*, March 1968, 'Lutheran Masses' by Paul Steinitz, for a discussion of these works.

3: PERFORMERS AND INSTRUMENTS

1 Burney, II, p.78.
2 Quoted in David and Mendel, p.123.
3 Ibid, p.120.
4 Information given in Chailley.
5 David and Mendel, p.124.
6 Donington, p.68.
7 Burney, II, p.78.
8 Geiringer, p.349.

4: THE TEXTS OF BACH'S PASSIONS

1 The St Luke Passion is almost certainly not by J.S. Bach, although it was published in volume XLV of the Bach Gesellschaft edition: scholars are nearly unanimous about this, but in any case the music is very unlike anything that Bach ever composed, even in his most immature years.
2 See *Bach Gesamtausgabe* XX (2) (Rust), *Bach Jahrbuch*, 1939 (Schering), and *Bach Jahrbuch*, 1940–48 (Smend) for full discussions of this subject.
3 Edited by D. Hellmann, Hänssler edition, Stuttgart.
4 Conductor, the present writer.
5 See Bibliography.
6 Terry, *The Music of Bach*, p.81.
7 Terry, *J.S. Bach*, p.145.
8 For more detailed information about the origin and use of chorales in Bach's Passions, together with other interesting information, see Terry, *Bach's Chorales*, Part 1.
9 Ibid, p.vi.
10 Ibid.
11 Smallman, 1970, p.91.
12 Blume, 1975, p.254.
13 Ibid, p.255.
14 Ibid, p.259.
15 Formerly attributed to Handel and published in the German Handel Society edition in Volume IX; there is also a vocal score edited by Harald Heilmann, Berlin, 1957.
16 Geiringer, p.197
17 Ibid, p.198.

5: THE MUSIC OF THE ST JOHN PASSION

1 Quoted by Schrade, pp.5–10.
2 Cf. A.T. Katz, *A Challenge to Musical Tradition*, London, 1947.
3 Geiringer, p.197. Cf. also Schweitzer, II, p.181.

6: THE MUSIC OF THE ST MATTHEW PASSION

1 Schweitzer, II, p.211.
2 Geiringer, p.201.
3 Schweitzer, p.229.

7: CHANGES MADE BY BACH IN THE ST JOHN AND ST MATTHEW PASSIONS

1 These changes and the reasons for them are discussed at length in Mendel, 'Traces of the Pre-History . . . ' (*Articles*), p.31ff.
2 Ibid, p.34.
3 Mendel, preface to *Neue Bach Ausgabe*, 1975.
4 Mendel, 'Traces of the Pre-History . . . ', p.42.
5 Mendel, preface to *Neue Bach Ausgabe*.
6 Cf. Mendel, 'Traces of the Pre-History . . . ' (*Articles*), with his subsequent complementary article in the *Journal of the American Musicological Society* and his later views in the preface to the miniature score of the *Neue Bach Ausgabe*, written in December 1974.
7 Dürr, preface to *Neue Bach Ausgabe*, 1972.
8 *Bach Jahrbuch*, 1949–50, p.96.
9 Mendel, 'Traces of the Pre-History . . .', p.44.
10 *Bach Jahrbuch*, 1928.
11 Geiringer, p.66.

8: PERFORMANCES AND PERFORMANCE STYLES

1 Quoted in Blume, 1950.
2 See Bibliography. London, p.68.
3 Quoted in C.H. Bitter, *Johann Sebastian Bach*, Berlin, 1865 and 1881, II, p.58.
4 Blume, 1950, p.25.
5 Rifkin, 'The Chronology of Bach's St Matthew Passion', *Musical Quarterly*, LXI, 1975, pp.360ff.
6 Donald Mintz (*Articles*, 1950), p.204.
7 Ibid, p.207.

8 Cf. Articles on the St Matthew Passion by A.B. Marx in Jahrgang No.9 of the *Allgemeine Zeitung* referred to by Mintz, pp.205ff.
9 Blume, 1950, p.44.
10 Quoted in Blume, 1950, p.45.
11 Devrient, p.14.
12 See Mintz, p.213.
13 Devrient, p.45.
14 Ibid, p.46.
15 Ibid. p.54.
16 Mintz, p.210.
17 Reported in Sebastian Hensel, translated Klingermann, *The Mendelssohn Family*, New York, 1882, I. p.169.
18 Devrient, pp.58ff.
19 Ibid, p.61.
20 Ibid, pp.62–63.
21 Ibid, p.75.
22 Blume,1950, p.54.
23 Ibid, p.56.
24 Robert Franz, *Johann Sebastian Bach's Passionsmusik nach dem Evangelisten Matthäus mit ausgeführtem Accompagnement*, Leipzig, 1903.
25 *Bach Jahrbuch*, 1904, pp.55ff.
26 Walters (*Articles*), p.180.
27 Walters, p.181.
28 De Wolfe Howe (*Articles*), p.180.
29 Walters, p.184.
30 De Wolfe Howe, pp.181ff.
31 Walters, p.179.
32 See Bibliography.
33 See F.G. Edwards, 'Bach's Music in England', *Musical Times*, October 1, 1896, p.654.
34 P. Scholes, *The Mirror of Music*, London, 1947, I, p.70.
35 Who this Hogarth was is not clear.
36 F.G. Edwards, p. 799.
37 *Musical Times*, April 1, 1854.
38 Quoted by W.A. Frost in a letter to *Musical Times*, February 1897.
39 *Musical Times*, May 1, 1870.
40 Announcement in the *Musical Standard*, April 5, 1873.
41 *Musical Standard*, March 30, 1872, p.169.
42 Ibid, p.161.
43 Scholes, pp.145–46.

APPENDIX: ORIGINS OF WORDS AND MELODIES IN THE CHORALES OF BACH'S
PASSIONS

1 For the information given in this Appendix I have drawn heavily on
   C.S. Terry's *Bach's Chorales*, Part I.

Bibliography

Editions of the Passions

Johannes-Passion: Bach Gesellschaft, Vol. XII, Leipzig, 1851–99.
Neue Bach Ausgabe, edited by A. Mendel, Bärenreiter, Kassel, 1973.
Matthäus-Passion, Bach Gesellschaft, Vol. IV, Leipzig, 1851–99.
Neue Bach Ausgabe, edited by A. Dürr, Bärenreiter, Kassel, 1972.

Books

Blume, F., translated by S. Godman, *Two Centuries of Bach*, London, 1950.
———— *Protestant Church Music, a History*, London and New York, 1975.
Boult, A. and Emery, W., *The St Matthew Passion, Its Preparation and Performance*, London, 1949.
Burney, C., *Present State of Music in Germany*, London, 1773.
Chailley, J., *Les Passions de J.S. Bach*, Paris, 1963.
Chiapusso, J., *Bach's World*, Bloomington and London, 1968.
David, H.T. and Mendel, A., *The Bach Reader*, London and New York, 1946; revised edition, 1967.
Devrient, E., translated by N. Macfarren, *My Recollections of Felix Mendelssohn-Bartholdy*, London, 1869.
Dickinson, A.E.F., *The Art of J.S. Bach*, revised edition, London, 1950.
Donington, R., *A Performer's Guide to Baroque Music*, London, 1973; New York, 1974.
Dürr, A., *Matthäus-Passion* in *Neue Bach Ausgabe*, Kassel, 1972; including Preface.
Forkel, J.N., translated by C.S. Terry, *The Life, Art and Works of J.S. Bach. For patriotic admirers of German Musical Art*; original edition, Leipzig, 1802; English edition, London, 1920.
Geiringer, K. and Geiringer, I., *John Sebastian Bach, the Culmination of an Era*, New York, 1966; London, 1967.
Grew, E.M. and S., *Bach* (Master Musicians Series), London, 1947; New York, 1949.

Mann, W., *Introduction to the Music of Bach*, London, 1950.

Mendel, A., Preface to *Johannes-Passion, Neue Bach Ausgabe*, Kassel, 1973 (miniature score 1975).

Nickel, T.H. (ed.), *The Little Bach Book*, Valparaiso, Ind., 1950.

Parry, C.H.H., *Johann Sebastian Bach*, London, 1909.

Pirro, A., translated by M. Savill, *J.S. Bach*, New York, 1957; London.

Schmieder, W., *Bach-Werke-Verzeichnis*, Leipzig, 1950.

Scholes, P., *The Mirror of Music*, two volumes, London and New York, 1947.

Schrade, L., *Bach, the Conflict between the Sacred and the Secular*, New York, 1955.

Schweitzer, A., *J.S. Bach*, two volumes, London, 1911; New York.

Smallman, B., *The Background of Passion Music*, revised edition, New York, 1970; London, 1971.

Spitta, C.J.P., translated by Bell and Fuller-Maitland, *Johann Sebastian Bach*, three volumes, London, 1899.

Terry, C.S., *The Music of Bach*, London and New York, 1933.

---- *J.S. Bach, A Biography*, London and New York, 1928.

---- *Bach, The Passions*, Musical Pilgrim, London and New York, 1926.

---- *Bach's Orchestra*, 1932; revised by Thurston Dart, London and New York, 1958.

---- *Bach, the Historical Approach*, London, 1930.

---- *Bach's Chorales* (Part I especially), Cambridge, 1915.

Wesley, S., edited by E. Wesley, *Bach Letters* (*Letters of Samuel Wesley to Mr Jacobs*), London, 1876.

Williams, A., *Bach*, London, 1900 and 1934.

Articles

Mendel, 'Traces of the Pre-History of Bach's St John and St Matthew Passions' in *O. Deutsch: Festschrift zum 80 Geburtstag, Kassel, 1963*.

Mintz, D., 'Some Aspects of the Bach Revival', *Musical Quarterly*, XL, 1950.

Rifkin, J., 'The Chronology of Bach's St Matthew Passion', *Musical Quarterly*, LXI, 1975.

Steinitz, P., 'German Choral Music', in *New Oxford History of Music*, V, London, 1975.

Walters, R., 'Bach at Bethlehem', *Musical Quarterly*, XXI, 1935.

Wolfe Howe, M.A. De, 'Venite in Bethlehem', *Musical Quarterly*, XXVIII, 1942.

See also: *Bach Jahrbuch*, 1928, 1939–1950. *Musical Times*, April 1954; May 1970; October 1896; February 1897. *Musical Standard*, April 23, 1870; March 30, 1972; April 12, 1873.

Discography

compiled from the Classical Gramophone Catalogue December 1977

St John Passion	*UK*	*USA*
Gillesberger conducting the t'Hoff Choir, Vienna Concentus Musicus, with Villisech, Scheewein, Equiluz and Egmond.	FK6 35018 (1967)	Telefunken 3635018
Britten conducting the Wandsworth School Choir, English Chamber Orchestra, with Harper, Hill, Hodgson, Pears, Burgess, Tobin, Thompson, Tear, Shirley-Quirk and Howell.	SET 351–3 (1972)	London Records OSA 13104
Willcocks conducting the Choir of King's College Cambridge, Philomusica of London, with Harwood, Watts, Pears, Young, Ward and Alan.	GOS 628–30 (1973) (English)	
Münchinger conducting the Stuttgart Chamber Orchestra and Chorus, with Ameling, Koehnlein-Goebel, Hamari, Ellenbeck, Hollweg, Isenhardt, Ackermann and Ahrans.	SET 590–2 (1975)	
St Matthew Passion		
Jacques conducting the Bach Choir and Orchestra, with Suddaby, Ferrier, Greene, Clinton, Cummings and Parsons.	D4 2D3 (1948) (Reissued 1977) (English)	
Richter conducting the Munich Bach Choir and Orchestra, with Fahberg, Seefried, Töpper, Haefliger, Engen, Fischer-Dieskau and Proebstl.	Archive 2712001 (1959)	DG ARC 2712 001

	UK	USA
Klemperer conducting the Hampstead Church Choir, Philharmonia Chorus and Orchestra, with Schwarzkopf, Evans, Ludwig, Watts, Pears, Brown, Berry, Gedda, Case, Krause and Fischer-Dieskau.	SLS 827 (1962)	Angel SCEX 3599
Münchinger conducting the Messthaler Choir, Stuttgart Philharmonic Orchestra, with Ameling, Hoffgen, Pears, Wunderlich, Blankenburg, Krause and Prey.	SET288 91 (1965)	London Records OSA 1431
Harnoncourt conducting the King's College Choir and Vienna Concentus Musicus, with Bowman, Esswood, Sutcliffe, Equiluz, Rogers, Egmond, Ridderbusch and Schopper.	HF6 35047 (1971)	Telefunken 4635047
Gottsche conducting the Abel Chorus and Heidelberg Chamber Orchestra, with Groschke, Wenkel, Ellenbeck, Juhani and Koenig.	BACH1103–6 (1971)	
Karajan conducting the Vienna Singverein and Berlin Philharmonic Orchestra, with Janowitz, Ludwig, Laubenthal, Schreier, Berry, Diakov and Fischer-Dieskau.	DG2720 070 (1973)	DG2711 012

Index